ES

ARCHITECTURE IN SPAIN

PHILIP JODIDIO

TASCHEN

HONG KONG KÖLN LONDON LOS ANGELES MADRID PARIS TOKYO

CANARY ISLANDS

INTRODUCTION

OPENING THE GATES OF INVENTION

It might surprise some to hear that Spain has a vibrant culture of contemporary architecture. Perhaps most clearly marked by the famous Barcelona Pavilion designed by Ludwig Mies van der Rohe for the 1929 International Exposition, the emergence of modernity was surely delayed by the Spanish Civil War, and the first period of the rule of Francisco Franco. And yet, it was in 1929 that Josep Lluís Sert graduated from the Barcelona School of Architecture. Sert went on to work in the office of Le Corbusier and Pierre Jeanneret in Paris. He designed the Spanish Pavilion at the Paris World Fair (1937), in which Pablo Picasso's *Guernica* was exhibited, commemorating the Nazi assault on the town of Guernica on April 26, 1937. When the Spanish Republican government fell in 1939, Sert moved to the United States. From 1947 to 1956 he was the president of the CIAM (Congres Internationaux d'Architecture Moderne). Succeeding Walter Gropius in 1953 he was appointed dean of the Graduate School of Design and professor of architecture at Harvard University, a position he held until his retirement in 1969. Sert's lyrical modernity is still quite visible in such realizations as the Fundación Joan Miró (Barcelona, 1975) or the Fondation Maeght (Saint-Paul-de-Vence, 1968).

BREAKING DOWN THE BARRIERS

Although the recent flowering of Spanish culture is seen as having begun with the death of Franco in 1975, the regime actually began to open to the world in the 1950s. Architects such as Coderch & Valls or Bohigas & Martorell brought the premises of modern design to residences, both individual and collective. The Spanish Pavilion at the 1958 Brussels Expo (Corrales & Molezún) announced that Iberian architecture had at last entered the postwar period. Even the Catholic Church, with structures such as the Almendrales Church (José María García de Paredes, Madrid, 1964) participated in the new openness. Larger-scale Modernist buildings sprang up with a certain economic prosperity in the 1960s, as witnessed by the Torres Blancas Apartment Building in Madrid for example (Francisco Javier Saenz de Oiza, 1968). Original personalities like Cesar Manrique Cabrera also marked this Spanish discovery of modernity, still overshadowed by dictatorship. Born in Arrecife, Lanzarote, in 1919, Manrique participated in the Civil War on the side of Franco then studied painting in Madrid. He lived and worked in New York from 1964 to 1966 before returning to the Canary Islands. "When I returned from New York, I came with the intention of turning my native island into one of the most beautiful places on the planet, due to the endless possibilities that Lanzarote had to offer," said Manrique. He left a mark on Lanzarote with his architecture and gardens as well as his painting. A fervent defender of local, traditional architecture, Manrique integrated his own house in Taro de Tahíche into its volcanic surroundings while being fully aware of the potential of contemporary design. His early and consistent efforts to protect the environment and traditions of his native island and to build within and on its volcanic stone make him a pioneer of a very personal approach to 20th-century architecture.

SURREAL MONUMENTS TO THE NEW SPAIN

Ricardo Bofill, born in 1939 in Barcelona, is in many ways a symbol of the emergence of Spanish architecture onto the European stage. In 1963 he created a group of architects, engineers, planners, sociologists, writers, movie-makers, and philosophers and founded the Taller de Arquitectura. His 1975 conversion of an abandoned cement factory into the offices of the Taller (Sant Just Desvern, Barcelona) signaled the rise of Postmodern architecture not only in Spain but across the developed world. As Bofill describes it, "The factory, abandoned and partially in ruins, was a compendium of surrealist elements: stairs that climbed up to nowhere, mighty reinforced concrete structures that sustained nothing, pieces of iron hanging in the air, huge empty spaces filled nonetheless with magic." His words evoke not only the skilful blending of industrial forms with modern architecture, but also the underlying encounter with Spain's artistic and literary traditions. His Marca Hispánica monument on the border between France and Catalonia (La Junquera, Gerona, 1976) can be interpreted in various ways, but it was built on the rubble of the highway linking Spain to the rest of Europe, a symbol in itself.

Although it is something of a coincidence, the opening of Spain to Europe and its adhesion to the European Community in 1986 was marked by the reconstruction of Mies van der Rohe's Barcelona Pavilion (demolished in 1930) on its original site by the architects Ignasi de Solà-Morales, Cristian Cirici and Fernando Ramos acting under the impetus first given in 1980 by Oriol Bohigas, then head of the Urban Planning Department of the Barcelona City Council. This exemplary reconstruction of an iconic structure, linking Spain to the roots of modernism could certainly be seen as a clear symbol of the country's bright European future.

EURO CHIC GETS OFF THE BOAT IN BILBAO

With the emergence of architects such as Rafael Moneo, first widely published with his National Museum of Roman Art (Mérida, 1985), or in a very different vein Santiago Calatrava, an expatriate native of Valencia, contemporary Spanish architecture began to take on the burgeoning international activity and reputation that it has today. Events such as the 1992 Barcelona Olympics or Expo '92 in Seville brought forth not only a new reservoir of local talents, but also attracted well-known foreign architects like Norman Foster (Collserola Tower, Barcelona, 1992) to the country. In 1995, Richard Meier inserted one of his trademark white designs into what had been a rather dark monastic enclave in Barcelona (Museum of Contemporary Art). This phenomenon has taken hold to such an extent that many of the most significant new buildings in the country from Herzog & de Meuron's Forum 2004 (Barcelona) to Jean Nouvel's Agbar Tower (Barcelona, 2005) or the Frenchman's controversial extension to the Reina Sofia Museum in Madrid (2005) are indeed the work of outsiders. Frank Gehry's 1998 Bilbao Guggenheim remains one of the most significant works of international contemporary architecture, and of course fueled the country's reputation for being open to innovative designs; while Los Angeles dithered over Gehry's finally complete Disney Concert Hall. With ongoing projects such as Peter Eisenman's large City of Culture of Galicia, the significant presence of foreigners in some of the country's most prestigious architectural settings is assured. The variety of these new buildings, and their apparent lack of any very specifically "Spanish" characteristics, despite architects' protestations to the contrary, does raise the issue of just why Spain has become such a hotbed of contemporary architecture.

CONSTRUCTION GETS REAL

The power of the emergence of Spain on the international architectural scene was noted by New York's Museum of Modern Art in a recent exhibition ("On-Site, New Architecture in Spain," February 12–May 1, 2006). Architecture curator Terry Riley noted, in the exhibition catalogue, that "in the last twenty years, the country has undertaken the most extensive building and rebuilding of its civil infrastructure since the Romans unified the Iberian Peninsula with roadways and aqueducts during the reign of Augustus. In recent years, the Spanish construction industry has eclipsed tourism and led all the other basic economic sectors. Rather than conforming to tourists' expectations, the recent wave of construction in Spain—much of which has been devoted to civil works—reflects a new sense of self-definition." Riley underlines the inherent diversity of Spain's regions, reflected in specific architectural terms in locations from Galicia to Catalonia and even to distant Tenerife. He also points out the widespread desire to return to a certain veracity in design, perhaps as opposed to the Postmodern wave so aptly represented by Bofill.

The projects selected for this book attempt to give only a broad overview of the work of Spanish architects in their country in the most recent period. Only work in Spain by Spanish architects has been retained, although figures like Santiago Calatrava have more of a base outside the country than within. There is no attempt to prove that a given style has come to dominate; indeed, it is the very variety of contemporary architecture that makes this selection both surprising and instructive. Well-known figures such as Moneo are accompanied here by figures who remain outside the mainstream, like Santiago Cirugeda.

The complex layering that often accompanies Spanish architecture, particularly in urban settings, might best be represented here by the rehabilitation of the Santa Caterina Market (Barcelona, 1997–2005). Designed by Enric Miralles and Benedetta Tagliabue, the work was completed after the death of Miralles in 2001 by their firm EMBT. The meteoric rise of Enric Miralles was cut short by his untimely death, but his unusual style, perhaps related in some instances to the "Deconstructivist" mode, and expressed in works such as the Igualada Cemetery Park (Barcelona, 1985–92), or the Olympic Archery Ranges, Barcelona (1989–91), had a strong impact around the world. His most significant posthumous work, the Scottish Parliament in Edinburgh, Scotland (1998–2004) was plagued by cost overruns and remarkable complexity, yet Miralles still incarnates the real emergence of Spain onto the international forefront of architecture. The Santa Caterina Market features a colorful mosaic roof made of more than 300 000 ceramic tiles, and reuses the original Neoclassical structure while introducing modern elements such as 42-meter steel arches. "We propose a model in which it is not so easy to distinguish between rehabilitation and new construction," say the architects.

RING AROUND THE BULLRING

A number of the projects published here share a strong concern for their attachment to the land of Spain or to some of its architectural traditions. This is no longer in any sense a matter of belated Postmodernism, but one of thoughtful reuse of historic sites or materials that recall the past, without imitating it. An attractive example of this tendency is the Badajoz Conference Center and Auditorium (1999-2006) by the architects Selgas Cano. Here, extremely modern polyester or Plexiglas rings define the limits of a circular structure with a 75-meter central void. The sense of this form and of the empty heart of the building is directly related to the fact that a bullring had occupied the location, itself set into a pentagonal 17th-century fortress. The modern materials employed render the historic implications of the site apparent without delving into any kind of pastiche. The fact that they also make a functional conference center out of such a strong form testifies to the talent of the architects.

A different kind of contextualism is expressed by the architect Josep Llinàs in his Jaume Fuster Library (Barcelona, 2001-05) where the building has become an intentional juncture between the city and the nearby Collserola mountains. Again the oblique angling of the building and its declared role of linking and movement from natural to urban environments does not lead to a purely "sculptural" or in other terms largely unusable design. Where Frank Gehry anchored a sculptural boat in Bilbao, Josep Llinàs makes his library emerge from both the land and the city. Another, quite different example of contemporary architecture that emerges from the earth, is the Magma Arts and Congress Centre (Adeje, Tenerife) completed in 2005 by Fernando Martín Menis and others. Thirteen geometrically shaped blocks form the convention complex, which is everywhere marked by the feeling of rough stone. On islands formed by volcanic activity, and earthquakes, these shapes are not innocent, but their abstraction avoids any overt attempt at "imitating" natural forms. Their emergence from the earth is powerfully modern, and expressed in a style that does not directly recall many other examples in contemporary architecture.

Often attached to the history of his land, Rafael Moneo recently completed the Art and Nature Center of the Beulas Foundation (Huesca, 1996-2005). The undulating surface of part of the building, set in agricultural fields, "dominates the scenery and relates to the nearby ridgelines—as if inspired by the rocky mounds of the *Mallos de Riglos*," according to the architect. While its exterior responds to its setting the very curves of the building make for unusual and effective interior exhibition spaces, once again rejecting any sense of superficial exterior manipulations. While much modernity, including the vaunted Barcelona Pavilion, rejected its surroundings, the new Spanish architecture appears to frequently emerge from its site, from the land itself, or from the urban environment.

A STEP AHEAD OF THE GAME

These trends in contemporary Spanish architecture appear to be contributing factors in the emergence of new voices, whose sophistication and intelligence in design will surely be noted far beyond the borders of the Iberian Peninsula very quickly. One young architect of already considerable reputation is Eduardo Arroyo, born in 1964 in Bilbao. His Levene House (San Lorenzo de El Escorial, Madrid, 2002–05) goes so far as to challenge the fashionable precepts of "green" architecture to place a respect for the natural setting before other issues. "For the concept of this home, we asked ourselves," he pointedly says, "whether we were capable of building something while maintaining the utmost respect for the natural surroundings, avoiding speaking about sustainability, alternative energy or ecology as a veneer for modernity and political correctness." Adopting the design to existing trees on the site and to the natural topography, Arroyo created an astonishingly original house, which surely has less to do with any specific Spanish tradition than to a universally comprehensible sense of architecture. The Levene House is the product of its site and of its owner's programmatic requirements, but Arroyo's architecture attains a unique level of contemporary achievement in architecture.

The variety present in contemporary Spanish architecture is one of its most attractive elements. An architect like Alberto Campo Baeza for example, born in Valladolid in 1946, gives the idea of minimalist simplicity a new intensity with such works as his Guerrero House (Cádiz, 2004–05). In this house, a pure white geometric object with seemingly impenetrable eight-meter walls gives way to courtyards bathed in light. The architect's earlier Caja General de Ahorros de Granada Headquarters (Granada, 1999–2001) took an equally reductive formal vocabulary and made abstract use of references to Roman architecture with its *impluvium* of light," or even to the columns of Granada Cathedral, showing that even a kind of minimalism can find strength and justification in the history of the country and its architecture.

So, too, the very color that may characterize ephemeral aspects of life in Spain, if not frequently its architecture, becomes, in the hands of some architects, a new element in their buildings. The MUSAC Contemporary Art Museum (León, 2002–04) by architects Emilio Tuñón and Luis Mansilla, is a veritable symphony of color on the outside, with unashamedly brilliant shades of glazing, and a much more tempered interior. So too the Els Colors Kindergarten (Manlleu, Barcelona, 2003–04) by RCR Aranda Pigem Vilalta Arquitectes takes on a variety of slightly more subtle colors, ranging from red to yellow, in a sort of "construction game" for children. Neither of these architectural firms have made the extensive use of color into a stylistic item, and this may be a good indication of the freedom that reigns in Spain after the middle of the first decade of the 21st century. RCR also designed a park recently (Rough Rock Park in Les Preses, Gerona, 2003–04) that covers a 250-hectare area in the 12 000-hectare Garrotxa Volcano Park. Declared a protected nature zone in 1982, Garrotxa bears the traces of long efforts to dig and farm the harsh landscape. The architects have inserted weathering steel walls that limit paths into this curious world of stone. In a sense they make art or architecture of a natural setting that is rich in the history of labor. They dig into the earth of Spain to draw a new meaning from its history.

The uninhibited inventiveness shown by RCR in two very different projects might well be the closest one can come to answering the question of why contemporary Spanish architecture is so rich and varied. The sum of many culturally varied regions, the country has opened itself to Europe and the rest of the world, in the process discovering that modernity need not turn its back on the past entirely. The projects selected in this book represent only a very small proportion of the interesting work being done in Spain, but like everywhere else "quality" architecture is exceptional, overwhelmed in quantity by the mediocrity that rules so much new construction. The architects of Spain, usually trained in their own country, have raised the standard for inventive design to one of the highest levels in Europe, and that in itself is a considerable event. Rebuilding the Barcelona Pavilion was a symbolic act, but its result, in the broadest sense, was not to bind Spanish architects to a fleeting Modernist past so much as to open the floodgates of invention.

EINLEITUNG

DIE TORE FÜR NEUES ÖFFNEN

Es mag manchen überraschen, wenn er hört, dass es in Spanien eine lebendige Szene zeitgenössischer Architektur gibt. Denn der Spanische Bürgerkrieg und vor allem der erste Abschnitt des Regimes von Francisco Franco haben die moderne Bewegung der 1920er-Jahre zunächst unterbrochen. Der Auftritt der Moderne ist vielleicht am eindeutigsten festzumachen an dem für die Weltausstellung 1929 von Mies van der Rohe entworfenen Barcelona-Pavillon. Im selben Jahr schloss Josep Lluís Sert sein Studium an der Escuela Superior de Arquitectura in Barcelona ab. Sert arbeitete in der Folge im Büro von Le Corbusier und Pierre Jeanneret in Paris. Er entwarf den spanischen Pavillon für die Weltausstellung in Paris im Jahr 1937, in dem Picassos Bild „Guernica" gezeigt wurde, das zum Gedenken an den Überfall der Nazis auf die Stadt Guernica am 26. April 1937 entstanden war. Als 1939 die Republik fiel, wanderte Sert in die Vereinigten Staaten aus. Von 1947 bis 1956 stand er als Präsident den CIAM (Congrès Internationaux d'Architecture Moderne) vor. Als Nachfolger von Walter Gropius wurde er 1953 zum Dekan der Graduate School of Design und zum Professor in Harvard berufen, eine Position, die er bis zu seinem Ruhestand 1969 innehatte. Serts lyrische Moderne ist in Bauten wie der Fundación Joan Miró (Barcelona 1975) und der 1968 entstandenen Fondation Maeght in St. Paul de Vence immer noch sehr präsent.

DIE SCHRANKEN ÜBERWINDEN

Zwar wird der Beginn der Blütezeit der spanischen Kultur häufig mit Francos Tod 1975 gleichgesetzt, doch sein Regime hatte bereits in den 1950er-Jahren begonnen, sich der Welt zu öffnen. Architekten wie Coderch & Valls oder Bohigas & Martorell führten jeder für sich und gemeinsam die Prämissen des modernen Designs in den Wohnhausbau ein. Dem für die Weltausstellung in Brüssel 1958 von Corrales & Molezún entworfenen spanischen Pavillon war anzusehen, dass auch für die spanische Architektur endlich die Nachkriegszeit begonnen hatte. Selbst die katholische Kirche beteiligte sich mit Bauten wie der 1964 in Madrid errichteten Iglesia de Almendrales von José María García de Paredes an der neuen Offenheit. In der Folge eines gewissen wirtschaftlichen Aufschwungs entstanden in den 1960er-Jahren größere modernistische Bauten wie beispielsweise 1968 in Madrid die Wohnanlage Torres Blancas von Francisco Javier Sáenz de Oíza. Außerdem prägten unabhängige Persönlichkeiten wie César Manrique Cabrera die noch immer von der Diktatur überschattete Entdeckung der Moderne in Spanien. Manrique, 1919 in Arrecife auf Lanzarote geboren, kämpfte im Bürgerkrieg auf Seiten Francos und studierte danach Malerei in Madrid. Von 1964 bis 1966 lebte er in New York, ehe er auf die Kanarischen Inseln zurückkehrte. „Als ich aus New York zurückkam, wollte ich meine heimatliche Insel Lanzarote dank ihrer unendlichen Möglichkeiten zum schönsten Ort der Erde machen", sagte Manrique. Mit seiner Architektur und den Gartenanlagen ebenso wie mit seiner Malerei hinterließ er sichtbare Spuren auf Lanzarote. Manrique, der leidenschaftlich für lokale, traditionelle Architektur eintrat, integrierte sein eigenes Wohnhaus in Taro de Tahíche in das vulkanische Umfeld, wiewohl er sich des Potenzials der Moderne durchaus bewusst war. Seine frühen, beharrlichen Bemühungen, die Umwelt sowie die Traditionen Lanzarotes zu schützen und im dortigen vulkanischen Gestein zu bauen, machten ihn zum Pionier einer sehr individuellen Einstellung zur Architektur des 20. Jahrhunderts.

SURREALE DENKMÄLER FÜR DAS NEUE SPANIEN

Der 1939 in Barcelona geborene Ricardo Bofill kann in vieler Hinsicht als Symbol für den Auftritt der Architektur Spaniens auf der europäischen Bühne gelten. 1963 versammelte er eine Gruppe von Architekten, Ingenieuren, Planern, Soziologen, Autoren, Filmemachern und Philosophen und begründete die Taller de Arquitectura (Architekturwerkstatt). Als er 1975 eine aufgelassene Zementfabrik zu den Büros der Taller (Sant Just Desvern, Barcelona) umbaute, leitete er nicht nur in Spanien, sondern überall in den westlichen Ländern den Aufstieg der Postmoderne ein. Bofill beschreibt das so: „Die verlassene, teilweise eingestürzte Fabrik stellte ein Kompendium surrealistischer Elemente dar: Treppen, die ins Nichts führten, imposante Stahlbetongefüge, die nichts trugen, Eisenteile, die in der Luft hingen, riesige, anscheinend leere und doch von Magie erfüllte Räume." Seine Worte rufen nicht nur die geschickte Verschmelzung industrieller Formen mit moderner Architektur wach, sondern ebenso die unterschwellige Begegnung mit Spaniens künstlerischen und literarischen Traditionen. Sein Denkmal Marca Hispánica auf der Grenze zwischen Frankreich und Katalonien (La Junquera, Girona, 1976) lässt sich unterschiedlich deuten, jedenfalls entstand es auf dem Aushub der Autobahn, die Spanien mit dem übrigen Europa verbindet, ein Symbol an sich.

Obgleich wohl eher zufällig, fiel die Öffnung Spaniens nach Europa und sein Beitritt zur Europäischen Gemeinschaft im Jahr 1986 zusammen mit der Rekonstruktion von Mies van der Rohes 1930 zerstörtem Barcelona-Pavillon an seinem originalen Standort. Ausgeführt wurde der Nachbau von den Architekten Ignasi de Solà-Morales, Cristian Cirici und Fernando Ramos, die eine Idee umsetzten, die 1980 von Oriol Bohigas, dem damaligen Leiter des Amts für Stadtplanung von Barcelona, aufgebracht worden war. Diese beispielhafte Rekonstruktion einer Ikone der Moderne, die Spanien mit den Wurzeln des Modernismus in Verbindung bringt, könnte sicher als deutliches Symbol für die leuchtende europäische Zukunft des Landes verstanden werden.

EUROSCHICK HEBT IN BILBAO AB

Mit dem Auftreten von Architekten wie Rafael Moneo, der mit dem 1985 erbauten Nationalmuseum für römische Kunst in Mérida debütierte, oder in völlig anderer Ausprägung, dem in Valencia gebürtigen und inzwischen im Ausland ansässigen Santiago Calatrava, begann die spanische Architektur international zu wirken und sich ihre heutige Reputation zu erwerben. Ereignisse wie die Olympischen Spiele 1992 in Barcelona oder die im gleichen Jahr stattfindende Expo in Sevilla verhalfen nicht nur einheimischen Talenten zum Durchbruch, sondern brachten renommierte auswärtige Architekten wie Norman Foster (Collserola-Turm, Barcelona, 1992) ins Land. 1995 fügte Richard Meier einen seiner charakteristischen weißen Bauten in eine vormals eher dunkle, klösterliche Enklave in Barcelona ein (Museu d'Art Contemporani de Barcelona). Dieses Phänomen griff in einem Maß um sich, dass es sich bei vielen der bedeutendsten neuen Bauten im Land, angefangen mit Herzog & de Meurons Forum 2004 in Barcelona bis zu Jean Nouvels Agbar-Turm von 2005, ebenfalls in Barcelona, oder auch dem 2005 entstandenen umstrittenen Erweiterungsbau des Franzosen für das Museo Reina Sofía in Madrid, um Werke auswärtiger Architekten handelt. Frank Gehrys Guggenheim-

Museum in Bilbao von 1998 bleibt eines der wichtigsten Werke internationaler zeitgenössischer Architektur und verstärkte natürlich den Eindruck, dass Spanien innovativen Entwürfen gegenüber aufgeschlossen ist, während man sich in Los Angeles lange nicht für Gehrys Disney-Konzerthalle entscheiden konnte. Mit laufenden Projekten wie Peter Eisenmans groß angelegter Cidade da Cultura de Galicia (CCG) bleibt die Präsenz ausländischer Architekten bei einigen der prestigeträchtigsten Architekturvorhaben gewährleistet. Die Vielfalt dieser neuen Bauten und das augenscheinliche Fehlen jeglicher spezifisch „spanischer" Merkmale – wenngleich die Architekten gerne das Gegenteil behaupten – wirft die Frage auf, weshalb Spanien zu einem solchen Eldorado zeitgenössischer Architektur wurde.

ES WIRD ERNST MIT DEM BAUEN

Kürzlich widmete das Museum of Modern Art in New York dem machtvollen Auftritt Spaniens auf der internationalen Architekturbühne eine Ausstellung („On-Site, New Architecture in Spain", 12.2.–1.5.2006). Kurator Terry Riley stellt im Katalog der Ausstellung fest: „Das Land hat in den letzten 20 Jahren den umfangreichsten Neu- und Umbau seiner zivilen Infrastruktur getätigt seit die Römer unter Augustus die iberische Halbinsel durch Straßen und Aquädukte einten. In den letzten Jahren löste die spanische Bauindustrie den Tourismus an der Spitze aller Wirtschaftszweige ab. Die jüngste Bauwelle in Spanien, von der ein Großteil staatliche Aufträge betraf, entspricht nicht so sehr den Erwartungen der Touristen, sondern spiegelt vielmehr ein neues Gefühl der Selbstbestimmung." Riley unterstreicht die Verschiedenheit der Regionen Spaniens, die sich von Galicien bis Katalonien und selbst im fernen Teneriffa in spezifischen Architekturbegriffen spiegelt. Darüber hinaus weist er auf den weit verbreiteten Wunsch hin, zu einer gewissen Wahrhaftigkeit des Entwerfens zurückzukehren, im Gegensatz zu der von Bofill so gekonnt vertretenen Postmoderne.

Die für diesen Band ausgewählten Projekte stellen lediglich den Versuch dar, über die neuesten Bauwerke spanischer Architekten in ihrem Land einen weitgefassten Überblick zu geben. Nur Werke spanischer Architekten in Spanien wurden aufgenommen, wenngleich Persönlichkeiten wie Santiago Calatrava außerhalb Spaniens häufiger tätig sind als innerhalb. Es wird nicht der Versuch unternommen, die Vorherrschaft einer bestimmten Stilrichtung nachzuweisen, sondern es ist im Gegenteil gerade die Vielfalt der zeitgenössischen Architektur, die diese Auswahl überraschend und aufschlussreich erscheinen lässt. Bekannte Architekten wie Moneo werden durch Personen wie Santiago Cirugeda ergänzt, die sich außerhalb des Mainstream bewegen.

Die komplexe Schichtung, häufig Bestandteil spanischer Architektur insbesondere im urbanen Kontext, kann hier vielleicht am besten anhand der Sanierung des Santa-Caterina-Marktes in Barcelona (1997–2005) veranschaulicht werden. Das von Enric Miralles und Benedetta Tagliabue konzipierte Projekt konnte erst nach dem Tod von Miralles (2001) von ihrem Büro EMBT fertig gestellt werden. Miralles' kometenhafter Aufstieg fand durch seinen vorzeitigen Tod ein frühes Ende, aber sein außergewöhnlicher Stil, der sich bisweilen auf den Dekonstruktivismus zu beziehen scheint und der in Projekten wie dem Friedhof Igualada

(Barcelona, 1985–92) oder der Olympischen Bogenschießanlage (1989–91) zum Ausdruck kommt, hat weltweit Auswirkungen. Sein bedeutendstes posthumes Werk, das schottische Parlament in Edinburgh (1998–2004), litt unter Budgetüberschreitungen und anderen beachtlichen Schwierigkeiten, und doch verkörpert Miralles das Erscheinen Spaniens an der Spitze der internationalen Architektur. Der Santa-Caterina-Markt zeichnet sich aus durch ein buntes Mosaikdach aus mehr als 300.000 Fliesen. Der ursprüngliche neoklassizistische Bau wird weiter genutzt, während moderne Elemente wie Stahlbögen mit 42 m Spannweite zum Einsatz kommen. Die Architekten sprechen von „einer Bauform, bei der es nicht leicht fällt, zwischen Sanierung und Neubau zu unterscheiden".

RING UM DIE STIERKAMPFARENA

Bei einer Reihe der hier gezeigten Projekte spielt ihre Bindung an Spanien oder eine seiner architektonischen Traditionen eine wichtige Rolle. Es geht dabei nicht um einen Fall verspäteter Postmoderne, sondern um die durchdachte Wiederverwendung historischer Orte oder von Materialien, die an die Vergangenheit erinnern, ohne sie zu imitieren. Ein gelungenes Beispiel ist das 1999 bis 2006 erbaute Kongresszentrum mit Auditorium in Badajoz von den Architekten Selgas und Cano. Hochmoderne Polyester- oder Plexiglasringe bezeichnen die Grenzen einer kreisförmigen Anlage mit einem zentralen leeren Raum mit einem Durchmesser von 75 m. Die Anmutung dieser Form und des leeren Zentrums erinnert daran, dass sich hier eine Stierkampfarena befand, die man ihrerseits in eine fünfeckige Bastion aus dem 17. Jahrhundert eingefügt hatte. Die modernen Materialien spiegeln die historischen Implikationen des Schauplatzes, ohne als Nachahmung zu wirken. Die Tatsache, dass aus einer derartig markanten Form ein funktionierendes Kongresszentrum wurde, zeugt vom Talent der Architekten.

Bei der von Josep Llinàs entworfenen Biblioteca Jaume Fuster (Barcelona, 2001–05), die als bewusstes Bindeglied zwischen Stadt und nahe gelegenen Collserola-Bergen fungiert, kommt eine andere Spielart von Kontextualismus zum Ausdruck. Die schräge Winkligkeit des Gebäudes und seine erklärte Rolle als Mittler zwischen natürlichem und urbanem Kontext führen nicht zu einer rein „skulpturalen" oder in anderer Hinsicht weitgehend unbrauchbaren Formgebung. Wo Frank Gehry in Bilbao eine Schiffsskulptur vor Anker gehen ließ, lässt Josep Llinàs seine Bibliothek gleichermaßen aus der Landschaft und der Stadt hervortreten.

Ein ganz anderes Beispiel zeitgenössischer Architektur, das aus der Erde aufsteigt, ist das 2005 fertig gestellte Kongresszentrum Magma Arte & Congresos (Adeje, Teneriffa) von Fernando Martin Menis und anderen. 13 geometrisch geformte Blöcke bilden den Komplex, der rundum von rauen Steinoberflächen geprägt ist. Auf Inseln, die durch vulkanische Aktivitäten und Erdbeben entstanden, sind solche Formen nicht fremd, aber dank ihrer Abstraktion vermeiden sie jeglichen offenkundigen Versuch, natürliche Formen nachzuahmen. Die Art, in der sie aus dem Erdboden „wachsen", ist radikal modern in einem Stil, für den es in der zeitgenössischen Architektur nur wenig Vergleichbares gibt.

Rafael Moneo stellte 2005 das 1996 begonnene Zentrum für Kunst und Natur der Fundación Beulas in Huesca fertig, das inmitten landwirtschaftlich genutzter Felder steht. Die wellenförmige Oberfläche eines Teils des Gebäudes beherrscht dem Architekten zufolge „die Gegend und nimmt Bezug auf die nahe gelegenen Hügelketten – als wäre es von den felsigen Erhebungen der Mallos de Riglos inspiriert". Während der Außenbau auf seinen Standort reagiert, ist es gerade die Wellenform des Gebäudes, die im Inneren ungewöhnliche, attraktive Ausstellungsräume entstehen lässt und wiederum jeglichem Eindruck oberflächlicher Effekthascherei eine Absage erteilt. Während ein großer Teil der Moderne, darunter der vielgerühmte Barcelona-Pavillon, seine Umgebung ignorierte, scheint die neue spanische Architektur häufig aus ihrem ländlichen oder städtischen Standort hervorzugehen.

EINEN SCHRITT VORAUS

Diese Tendenzen in der aktuellen Architektur Spaniens gehen anscheinend einher mit dem Aufkommen neuer Stimmen, deren anspruchsvolle, intelligente Entwürfe man gewiss bald jenseits der spanischen Grenzen anerkennen wird. Ein junger Architekt, der sich bereits heute eines beträchtlichen Renommees erfreut, ist Eduardo Arroyo, der 1964 in Bilbao geboren wurde. Bei seiner Casa Levene (San Lorenzo de El Escorial, 2002–05) geht er so weit, die in Mode gekommenen Gebote „grüner" Architektur in Frage zu stellen, um den Respekt vor dem naturgegebenen Umfeld wichtiger zu bewerten als alle anderen Aspekte. „Bei der Konzeption dieses Hauses fragten wir uns", so seine pointierte Anmerkung, „ob wir in der Lage sein würden, etwas zu bauen und dabei den größtmöglichen Respekt für die umgebende Natur zu bewahren; außerdem wollten wir die Erwähnung von Nachhaltigkeit, alternativer Energie oder Ökologie als Fassade für Modernität und ‚political correctness' vermeiden." Indem er die Größe des Hauses den vorhandenen Bäumen und der Topografie des Geländes anpasste, schuf Arroyo ein erstaunlich originelles Haus, das weit weniger mit spezifisch spanischen Traditionen zu tun hat, als mit einem universell verständlichen Gespür für Architektur. Die Casa Levene orientiert sich an ihrem Standort und den programmatischen Forderungen ihres Besitzers, und Arroyo stößt mit diesem Haus an die Spitze der zeitgenössischen Architektur vor.

Die in der derzeitigen Architektur Spaniens anzutreffende Vielfalt ist einer ihrer reizvollsten Aspekte. So verhilft beispielsweise der 1946 in Valladolid geborene Alberto Campo Baeza dem Eindruck minimalistischer Schlichtheit mit Werken wie seiner Casa Guerrero (Cádiz, 2004–05) zu neuer Intensität. Hinter den scheinbar undurchdringlichen, 8 m hohen Mauern dieses rein weißen, geometrischen Objekts befinden sich in Licht getauchte Innenhöfe. Für die zuvor gebaute Caja General de Ahorros de Granada (Granada, 1999–2001) verwendete er eine ähnlich reduzierte Formensprache und stellte mit dem „Lichtimpluvium" abstrakte Bezüge zur römischen Architektur her. Denkbar ist auch eine Anspielung auf die Säulen der Kathedrale von Granada, womit bewiesen wäre, dass selbst eine Form des Minimalismus Stärke und Rechtfertigung in der Geschichte des Landes und seiner Architektur finden kann.

Ebenso wird eben jene Farbigkeit, die flüchtige Aspekte des Lebens in Spanien, wenn auch nicht häufig seine Architektur kennzeichnet, in den Händen einiger Architekten zu einem neuen Element ihres Bauens. Das von den Architekten Emilio Tuñón und Luis Mansilla erbaute Kunstzentrum MUSAC (León, 2002–04) zeigt auf seiner Außenseite eine wahre Farbsinfonie mit unverhohlen leuchtend farbigen Glasflächen, während das Interieur weit gemäßigter ist. So macht sich auch der Kindergarten Els Colors (Manlleu, Barcelona, 2003–04) von RCR Aranda Pigem Vilalta Arquitectes eine Auswahl etwas subtilerer Farbtöne zunutze, die bei einer Art „Baukasten" für Kinder von Rot bis Gelb reichen. Keines der beiden Architekturbüros machte eine Stilfrage aus dem extensiven Einsatz von Farbe, und dies mag als gutes Zeichen für die in Spanien herrschende künstlerische Freiheit zu werten sein. RCR zeichnet darüber hinaus für die Anlage eines 250 ha großen Parks verantwortlich (Parc de Pedra Tosca in Les Preses bei Girona, 2003–04), der ein Teil des 12 000 ha umfassenden Parque Natural de la Zona Volcánica de la Garrotxa ist. Das 1982 zum Naturschutzgebiet erklärte Areal ist gezeichnet von den langjährigen Bemühungen, die karge Landschaft umzugraben und landwirtschaftlich zu nutzen. Die Architekten zogen in diese seltsame Welt aus Stein witterungsbeständige Stahlwände ein, mit denen sie Pfade bezeichneten. In gewissem Sinn verwandelten sie eine an Arbeitsgeschichte reiche Naturlandschaft in Kunst oder Architektur. Sie graben in der Erde Spaniens, um aus seiner Geschichte neue Bedeutung zu extrahieren.

Möglicherweise ist der von RCR bei zwei sehr unterschiedlichen Projekten demonstrierte ungezügelte Einfallsreichtum die beste Antwort auf die Frage, weshalb sich die zeitgenössische Architektur Spaniens so ideenreich und vielfältig darstellt. Das Land als Summe vieler kulturell unterschiedlicher Regionen hat sich zu Europa und der übrigen Welt hin geöffnet und dabei festgestellt, dass die Moderne nicht zwangsläufig eine völlige Abkehr von der Vergangenheit bedeutet. Die für dieses Buch ausgewählten Projekte stellen nur einen sehr kleinen Teil der in Spanien entstehenden interessanten Bauwerke dar. Allerdings ist auch hier qualitätvolle Architektur die Ausnahme, die zahlenmäßig von der Menge der mediokren Neubauten weit übertroffen wird. Die zumeist im eigenen Land ausgebildeten spanischen Architekten haben den Standard innovativen Entwerfens europaweit mit auf das höchste Niveau gebracht, und das ist an sich schon eine beachtliche Entwicklung. Der Nachbau des Barcelona-Pavillons stellte einen symbolischen Akt dar, der jedoch nicht zur Folge hatte, dass spanische Architekten sich im weitesten Sinn auf einen vergänglichen Modernismus festlegten, sondern der im Gegenteil die Schleusentore für Neues öffnete.

INTRODUCTION

OUVRIR LES VANNES DE L'INVENTION

Certains seront peut-être surpris de découvrir que l'Espagne possède une culture de l'architecture contemporaine aussi dynamique. Brillamment saluée en 1929 par le fameux Pavillon de Barcelone conçu par Ludwig Mies van der Rohe pour l'Exposition universelle, l'apparition de la modernité fut malheureusement retardée par la Guerre civile et la première partie du « règne » de Francisco Franco. La même année, José Luis Sert sort diplômé de l'École d'architecture de Barcelone. Il part travailler à Paris auprès de Le Corbusier et de Pierre Jeanneret, puis conçoit le Pavillon espagnol pour l'Exposition universelle de Paris 1937 dans lequel le *Guernica* de Picasso rappelle le bombardement par les nazis de la petite ville de Guernica le 26 avril 1937. À la chute du gouvernement républicain espagnol, en 1939, il émigre aux États-Unis. De 1947 à 1956, il préside les Ciam (Congrès internationaux d'architecture moderne) et, en 1953, succède à Walter Gropius au poste de Doyen de la Graduate School of Design d'Harvard avant d'y devenir professeur d'architecture, fonction qu'il conserve jusqu'à sa retraite en 1969. En Europe, sa modernité lyrique s'est illustrée dans des réalisations comme la Fondation Joan Miró (Barcelone, 1975) ou la Fondation Maeght (Saint-Paul-de-Vence, 1968).

ROMPRE LES BARRIÈRES

Bien que l'on fasse souvent partir la renaissance de la culture espagnole de la mort de Franco en 1975, son régime avait commencé à s'ouvrir au monde dans les années 1950. Des architectes comme Coderch & Valls ou Bohigas & Martorell avaient déjà insufflé un esprit moderniste dans leurs projets de logements tant individuels que collectifs. Le Pavillon espagnol pour l'Exposition universelle de Bruxelles en 1958 (Corrales & Molezún) annonçait que l'architecture espagnole entrait enfin dans son après-guerre. Même l'église catholique, avec des réalisations comme l'église d'Almendrales (José María García de Paredes, Madrid, 1964), participait à cette ouverture. Des constructions modernistes de plus grande échelle apparurent, suscitées par la phase de prospérité économique des années 1960, dont l'immeuble résidentiel des Torres Blancas à Madrid (Francisco Javier Sáenz de Oíza, 1968). Des personnalités originales comme César Manrique Cabrera illustrèrent également cette ouverture à la modernité bien que le pays soit encore soumis à la dictature. Né à Arrecife (Lanzarote, 1919) Manrique avait participé à la Guerre civile du côté franquiste, puis étudié la peinture à Madrid. Il vécut et travailla à New York de 1964 à 1966 avant de revenir aux Canaries. « À mon retour de New York, je voulais faire de mon île natale de Lanzarote l'un des plus beaux endroits de la terre, si infinies étaient ses possibilités », écrivit-il. Il laissa sa marque sur l'île à travers son architecture, ses jardins mais aussi sa peinture. Fervent défenseur de l'architecture locale traditionnelle, il conçut sa propre maison de Taro de Tahiche intégrée à son environnement volcanique, mais parfaitement moderne d'esprit. Ses efforts précoces et constants pour protéger l'environnement et les traditions de l'île et pour construire à partir de et sur son sol volcanique font de lui le représentant d'une approche très personnelle de l'architecture du xxᵉ siècle.

MONUMENTS SURRÉALISTES À L'ESPAGNE NOUVELLE

Ricardo Bofill, né en 1939 à Barcelone, est à de nombreux égards un symbole de l'émergence de l'architecture espagnole sur la scène européenne. Son agence, le Taller de Arquitectura, créée en 1963, réunissait des architectes, des ingénieurs, des urbanistes, des sociologues, des écrivains, des cinéastes et des philosophes. En 1965, sa conversion d'une ancienne cimenterie abandonnée en bureaux pour le Taller (Sant Just Desvern, Barcelone) signala l'apparition de l'architecture post-moderne en Espagne mais aussi dans l'ensemble du monde développé. Bofill décrit ainsi ce projet : « Cette cimenterie abandonnée et partiellement en ruine était un compendium d'éléments surréalistes : escaliers qui montaient nulle part, structures en béton lourdement armé qui ne soutenaient rien, morceaux de fer suspendus dans les airs, énormes espaces vides mais néanmoins pleins de magie. » Ces mots évoquent non seulement la fusion habile de formes industrielles et d'architecture moderne, mais aussi une rencontre non-dite avec les traditions littéraires et artistiques espagnoles. Son monument de la Marca Hispánica, à la frontière entre la France et l'Espagne (La Junquera, Gerona, 1976), peut être interprété de multiples façons, mais il se dresse au bord de l'autoroute qui relie enfin l'Espagne au reste de l'Europe, un symbole en soi.

Bien que ce soit sans doute une coïncidence, l'ouverture de l'Espagne vers l'Europe et son adhésion à la CEE, en 1986, s'accompagna de la reconstruction du pavillon de Barcelone de Mies van der Rohe (démoli en 1930) sur son site d'origine par les architectes Ignasi de Solà-Morales, Cristian Cirici et Fernando Ramos, dans le cadre d'un mouvement initié en 1980 par Oriol Bohigas, alors responsable du département de l'urbanisme de la Ville de Barcelone. Cette reconstruction exemplaire d'une réalisation iconique rattachant l'Espagne aux racines du modernisme était un symbole clair du brillant futur qui attendait le pays intégré à l'Europe.

EURO CHIC

C'est avec l'émergence d'architectes comme Rafael Moneo, abondamment publié à partir de l'inauguration de son Musée national d'art romain de Mérida (1985) ou, dans une veine très différente, Santiago Calatrava, expatrié mais né à Valence, que l'architecture espagnole contemporaine a commencé à établir sa réputation et remporter les contrats internationaux dont elle bénéficie aujourd'hui. Des événements comme les Jeux olympiques de Barcelone en 1992 ou l'Expo '92 à Séville ont révélé une mine de talents locaux, mais ont aussi attiré des architectes étrangers fameux dont Norman Foster (tour de Collserola, Barcelone, 1992). En 1995, Richard Meier a inséré dans un sombre quartier ancien de Barcelone son Musée d'art contemporain dans le style tout de blancheur qui a fait sa célébrité. Ce phénomène a pris une telle ampleur que beaucoup des réalisations nouvelles les plus significatives du pays, du Forum 2004 d'Herzog de Meuron (Barcelone) à la tour Agbar de Jean Nouvel (Barcelone, 2005) ou son extension controversée du Musée Reina Sofía à Madrid (2005), sont en fait l'œuvre de personnalités extérieures. Le Guggenheim de Frank Gehry à Bilbao (1998) reste l'une des œuvres les plus importantes de l'architecture contemporaine internationale et sa création a alimenté la réputation du pays pour son ouverture aux projets novateurs alors que Los Angeles discutait encore du Disney Concert Hall aujourd'hui enfin achevé.

Avec des projets en cours de chantier comme la vaste Cité de la culture de Galice (Cidade da Cultura de Galicia, CCG) de Peter Eisenman, la présence marquante d'étrangers dans certains des cadres architecturaux les plus prestigieux du pays est assurée. La variété de ces nouveaux bâtiments et leur manque apparent de toute caractéristique spécifiquement « espagnole », malgré les protestations du contraire de la part des architectes, soulèvent la question de savoir pourquoi l'Espagne est devenue un terreau aussi fertile pour l'architecture contemporaine.

LA PART DU ROI

La puissante émergence de l'Espagne sur la scène architecturale internationale a été confirmée par le Museum of Modern Art de New York dans une récente exposition intitulée « On-Site, New Architecture in Spain » (12 février-1er mai 2006). Le conservateur de l'architecture, Terry Riley fait remarquer dans le catalogue que : « ... au cours des vingt dernières années, le pays s'est lancé dans un des programmes de construction et de reconstruction de ses infrastructures civiles le plus complet depuis que les Romains unifièrent la péninsule ibérique par des voies et des aqueducs sous le règne d'Auguste. Récemment, l'industrie du bâtiment s'est taillée la part du roi. Elle a éclipsé le tourisme et arrive en tête de tous les secteurs économiques essentiels. Plutôt que de se cantonner aux attentes des touristes, la récente vague de constructions en Espagne – dont une grande part est consacrée à des bâtiments municipaux – reflète une nouvelle recherche de définition identitaire. » Riley souligne la diversité des régions espagnoles qui s'exprime en termes de spécificités architecturales, de la Galice à la Catalogne et jusqu'à la lointaine Tenerife. Il note également le désir repandu de retrouver une certaine authenticité conceptuelle, par opposition peut-être à la vague postmoderniste si habilement représentée par Bofill.

Les projets sélectionnés pour cet ouvrage se proposent de donner une large vue d'ensemble de la production des architectes espagnols dans leur pays au cours de la période récente. Seules leurs interventions en Espagne ont été retenues bien que des personnalités comme Santiago Calatrava travaillent davantage à l'étranger. Il ne s'agit pas ici de prouver qu'un style domine plus que les autres, mais de montrer à quel point la variété même des réalisations présentées rend cette présentation à la fois surprenante et instructive. Des figures connues comme Moneo sont accompagnées d'autres qui restent en dehors des grands courants du moment, comme Santiago Cirugeda.

La stratification complexe qui accompagne souvent l'architecture espagnole, notamment dans le cadre urbain est particulièrement bien représentée ici par la réhabilitation du marché de Santa Caterina (Barcelone, 1997-2005). Conçu par Enric Miralles et Benedetta Tagliabue, ce projet a été achevé après le décès de Miralles en 2001 par leur agence commune, EMBT. L'ascension météorique de l'architecte a été brisée par sa mort précoce mais son style inhabituel, peut-être lié à certains égards à la mode « déconstructiviste », qui s'était exprimé dans des interventions comme le cimetière d'Igualada (Barcelone, 1985-92) ou le stade d'archerie olympique (Barcelone, 1989-91), ont eu un profond impact dans le monde. Son œuvre posthume la plus importante, le Parlement écossais à Édimbourg

(1995-2004), fut victime de dépassement de coûts et de son étonnante complexité, mais Miralles incarne toujours l'accession réelle de l'Espagne à l'avant-garde de l'architecture internationale. Le marché de Santa Caterina présente un toit en mosaïque polychrome de plus de 300 000 carreaux de céramique et réutilise la structure néo-classique d'origine tout en introduisant des éléments modernes comme des arcs en acier de 42 mètres. « Nous proposons un modèle qu'il n'est pas très facile de distinguer entre réhabilitation et construction neuve », ont précisé les architectes.

L'ANNEAU AUTOUR DE L'ARÈNE

Un certain nombre de ces projets montrent de fortes préoccupations communes pour l'attachement à la terre espagnole ou à certaines de ses traditions architecturales. Il ne s'agit en rien de quelque postmodernisme tardif mais d'une réutilisation réfléchie de sites ou de matériaux qui rappellent le passé sans pour autant l'imiter. Un séduisant exemple de cette approche est le Centre de conférences et auditorium de Badajoz (1999-2006) de l'architecte Selgas Cano. Ici, des anneaux d'aspect extrêmement moderne en polyester ou Plexiglas délimitent une construction circulaire autour d'un vide central de 75 mètres de diamètre. Le sens de cette forme et de la cour vide du bâtiment est directement lié à l'ancienne occupation du lieu par une arène, elle-même édifiée sur une forteresse pentagonale datant du XVIIIe siècle. Les matériaux modernes utilisés ici pointent ainsi le passé historique du site sans tomber pour autant dans un quelconque pastiche. Avoir pu réaliser un centre de conférences fonctionnel à partir d'une forme aussi puissante témoigne par ailleurs du talent des architectes.

Une approche contextualiste très différente s'exprime dans la Bibliothèque Jaume Fuster (Barcelone, 2001-05) de Josep Llinás dont le bâtiment établit intentionnellement un lien entre la ville et les proches collines de Collserola. L'inclinaison oblique du bâtiment et sa volonté de créer un lien dynamique entre l'environnement urbain et celui de la nature ne débouche pas pour autant sur un projet « sculptural » ou, en d'autres termes, largement inutilisable. Alors que Frank Gehry ancre son « bateau » sculptural à Bilbao, Josep Llinás fait surgir sa bibliothèque à la fois du sol et de la ville.

Un autre exemple d'architecture contemporaine utilisant cette émergence quasi géologique est celui du Magma Arte & Congresos (Adeje, Tenerife) achevé en 2005 par Fernando Martín Menis et une équipe de collaborateurs. Treize blocs géométriques constituent ce complexe dans lequel prédomine la pierre brute. Sur ces îles nées d'éruptions volcaniques et de tremblements de terre, ces formes ne sont pas innocentes, mais leur abstraction évite toute tentative « d'imitation » de celles de la nature. Leur surgissement du sol est puissamment moderne et s'exprime dans un style qui ne rappelle directement aucune autre réalisation contemporaine.

Se montrant très souvent attaché à l'histoire de son pays, Rafael Moneo a récemment achevé le Centre d'art et de nature de la Fondation Beulas (Huesca, 1996-2005). L'ondulation de la couverture d'une partie de ce bâtiment implanté au milieu des champs « domine le paysage et renvoie aux lignes de crêtes voisines, comme inspirées des éminences rocheuses des Mállos de Riglos », précise l'architecte. Si ce traitement de l'extérieur répond au cadre, ses courbes engendrent à l'intérieur des espaces d'exposition inhabituels et efficaces, tout en rejetant là encore toute impression de manipulation extérieure superficielle. Alors que la modernité du si vanté Pavillon de Barcelone rejetait son environnement, la nouvelle architecture espagnole semble fréquemment naître du site, de la terre elle-même ou de l'environnement urbain.

EN TÊTE

Ces tendances espagnoles constituent sans doute des facteurs qui contribuent à l'apparition de voix nouvelles dont la sophistication et l'intelligence conceptuelle seront certainement bientôt remarquées bien au-delà des frontières de la Péninsule. Un de ces jeunes architectes de réputation déjà considérable est Eduardo Arroyo, né en 1964 à Bilbao. Sa Maison Levene (San Lorenzo de El Escorial, près de Madrid, 2002-2005) va jusqu'à défier les préceptes à la mode de l'architecture « verte » et place le respect du cadre naturel avant toute chose. « Pour le concept de cette maison, nous nous sommes demandés si nous étions capables de construire quelque chose qui respecterait le plus possible l'environnement naturel, sans pour autant parler de développement durable, d'énergies alternatives ou d'écologie, ces « placages » de modernité et du politiquement correct. » L'architecte, en adoptant la topographie naturelle du terrain, avec la présence de ses arbres, a créé une maison étonnamment originale qui se rapproche moins d'une tradition spécifiquement espagnole que du sens universel de l'architecture. Elle est le produit de son site et du programme souhaité par son propriétaire, mais atteint ici, avec Arroyo, un niveau d'accomplissement spécifique en architecture contemporaine.

La variété de l'architecture espagnole d'aujourd'hui est l'un de ses éléments le plus attractifs. Un architecte comme Alberto Campo Baeza par exemple, né à Valladolid en 1946, donne à la simplicité minimaliste une intensité nouvelle comme on le constate dans des réalisations comme la Maison Guerrero (Cadix, 2004-05). Cet objet géométrique pur aux murs de huit mètres de haut apparemment impénétrables s'ouvre par des cours baignées de lumière. Sa Caja General de Ahorros de Granada (Grenade, 1999-2001), qui lui est antérieure, empruntait un vocabulaire tout aussi concis et des références abstraites à l'architecture romaine comme dans son « *impluvium* de lumière » ou les colonnes de la cathédrale de Grenade, ce qui montre que même une forme de minimalisme peut trouver sa force et sa justification dans l'histoire du pays et de son architecture.

Ainsi les couleurs qui caractérisent certains aspects éphémères de la vie en Espagne, et moins fréquemment son architecture, deviennent entre les mains de certains architectes une nouvelle composante de leurs projets. Le centre d'art MUSAC (León, 2002-04) par les architectes Emilio Tuñón et Luis Mansilla offre une symphonie de couleurs composée de vitrages aux nuances audacieuses qui contrastent avec un intérieur bien plus tempéré. De même, le jardin d'enfants Els Colors (Manlleu, Barcelone, 2003-04) par RCR Aranda Pigem Vilalta Arquitectes

fait appel à une variété de couleurs un peu plus subtiles, allant du rouge au jaune, comme dans une sorte de jeu de construction pour enfants. Aucune de ces agences ne fait de l'utilisation extensive de la couleur un élément de style et c'est peut-être là une bonne indication de la liberté qui règne en Espagne au milieu de la première décennie du XXIe siècle. RCR a également conçu, il y a peu, un parc (Parc de Pedra Tosca, Les Preses, Girona, 2003-04) sur 250 des 12 000 hectares du Parc du volcan de Garrotxa déclaré zone naturelle protégée en 1982, qui conserve les traces des efforts séculaires donnés à la culture de ce sol difficile. Les architectes y ont inséré des murs en acier patiné qui déterminent les cheminements dans cet étrange univers minéral. En un sens, ils créent de l'art ou de l'architecture à partir d'un cadre naturel mais riche de l'histoire du travail des hommes. Ils creusent dans la terre d'Espagne pour trouver un nouveau sens à son histoire.

L'inventivité sans inhibition dont témoigne RCR dans ces deux projets très différents nous rapproche sans doute de très près de la réponse à la question : pourquoi l'architecture espagnole contemporaine est-elle aussi riche et variée ? Composé de régions de cultures diverses, le pays s'est ouvert à l'Europe et au reste du monde et découvre actuellement que la modernité n'implique pas nécessairement de tourner le dos au passé. Les projets sélectionnés ici ne représentent qu'une très faible quantité des réalisations intéressantes trouvées aujourd'hui en Espagne, mais, comme partout, l'architecture de « qualité » est exceptionnelle, submergée en masse par la médiocrité qui gouverne tant de chantiers nouveaux. Les architectes espagnols, généralement formés dans leur pays, ont élevé les standards de l'inventivité à l'un des niveaux le plus haut d'Europe, ce qui est en soi un événement considérable. Reconstruire le Pavillon de Barcelone fut un acte symbolique cherchant non pas tant à lier les architectes espagnols à un passé moderniste qui s'était dérobé, qu'à ouvrir enfin les vannes de l'invention.

1

ÁBALOS & HERREROS

ABALOS & HERREROS
c/ Gran Via, 16, 3° C
28013 Madrid

Tel: +34 91 523 44 04
Fax: +34 91 523 45 53
e-mail: studio@abalos-herreros.com
Web: www.abalos-herreros.com

IÑAKI ÁBALOS VÁZQUEZ was born in San Sebastian in 1956 and completed his studies at the Escuela Técnica Superior de Arquitectura in Madrid (ETSAM). JUAN HERREROS GUERRA was born in San Lorenzo de El Escorial in 1958 and studied in the same school. Ábalos and Herreros have been working together since 1984. Iñaki Ábalos is a Chaired Professor, the Head Teacher of Design and Director of the Contemporary Techniques & Landscapes Laboratory, while Juan Herreros is Senior Lecturer and the Head of Teaching Unit Q in the department of projects at ETSAM, where they were previously professors of building design (1984-88). As they say, they have concentrated on the "amalgamation of natural and artificial elements" in their architecture. They published the book *Tower and Office, From Modernist Theory to Contemporary Practice* (MIT Press, 2003) about the role and impact of advanced building technologies in American architecture since World War II. Their built work includes: Parque Europa, a 455-unit Social Housing, Shop, and Garage complex, Palencia (1991-98); José Hierro Public Library, Usera, Madrid (1995-2003); a Recycling Plant for Urban Waste, Valdemingómez, Madrid (1998); Environmental Education Center and Offices, Arico, Tenerife (1998-2001); General Services Building for the University of Extremadura, Mérida, Badajoz (1999-2001); Biomethane and Compost Plant, Madrid (2003); Recycling Plant, Sant Adrià de Besòs (2000-04); Office Building and Eco-Museum for the Besòs Incinerator, Sant Adrià de Besòs (2000-04); Parc Litoral Nord-Est, Barcelona (2004). As well as the project published here, more recent work includes: exhibition space and show-room for a gallery, Madrid (2005); apartment and offices in Vitoria (2006); housing and parking in Orfila (2006); the Collection Building, Miami (under construction).

WOERMANN TOWER AND SQUARE
LAS PALMAS DE GRAN CANARIA 2001 - 05

DESIGNED BY ABALOS & HERREROS IN
COLLABORATION WITH CASARIEGO/GUERRA
CLIENT: Ferrovial Inmobiliaria
NET AREA: 23 370 m²
CONSTRUCTION COST OF TOWER AND OFFICE
BUILDING: €10 338 900
ARCHITECTS: Iñaki Abalos, Juan Herreros, Renata
Sentkiewicz, Joaquin Casariego, Elsa Guerra
COLLABORATING ARTIST: Albert Oehlen

The architects declare, "The Woermann Tower sets out to embody the illusions, desires and fantasies of a society that seeks to discover a compromise between nature and development, an intense form of life faithful to the landscape: another beauty." Aside from a public square on this sensitive site, the program requested of the architects included housing, offices, parking, retail spaces, and a library. The centrally located square was designed using Portuguese stone with the artist Albert Oehlen. A seven-story block to the south of the square includes offices and shops, while the 18-story, 60-meter structure to the north includes the library on the lower three floors, and residences above. The apartments are either four or five to a floor, and include one to four bedrooms. With a height of over three meters between each floor slab, the apartments are generous and offer views of the sea. The glass façades are protected from the sun by a system of *brise-soleils*, and vegetal motifs are etched into the glass making the "tower appear from the outside like a forest of shadows without scale." The architects compare the unusual shape of the tower to an "animated being nodding as if to contemplate the landscape," and bowing at the base "to yield to pedestrians."

Die Architekten erklären, „der Woermann-Turm schicke sich an, die Illusionen, Wünsche und Fantasien einer Gesellschaft zu verkörpern, die auf der Suche nach einem Kompromiss zwischen Natur und Entwicklung ist, nach einer intensiven Lebensform in Eintracht mit der Landschaft, nach einer anderen Schönheit." Neben einem öffentlichen Platz auf diesem heiklen Gelände, sah das von den Architekten verlangte Bauprogramm Wohnungen, Büros, Parkplätze, Ladengeschäfte sowie eine Bibliothek vor. Für die Gestaltung des zentralen Platzes verwendete der Künstler Albert Oehlen Stein aus Portugal. In einem siebenstöckigen Block an der Südseite des Platzes sind Büros und Läden untergebracht, während sich in dem 18-geschossigen, 60 m hohen Gebäude an der Nordseite auf den unteren drei Ebenen die Bibliothek und darüber Wohnungen befinden. Auf jeder Etage gibt es vier oder fünf Wohnungen, die jeweils mit einem bis vier Schlafzimmern ausgestattet sind. Da die Geschosshöhe über 3 m beträgt, wirken die Wohnungen großzügig und sie bieten Ausblicke aufs Meer. Die Glasfassaden werden durch ein System von Sonnenblenden vor der Hitze geschützt und die in das Glas geätzten vegetabilen Motive lassen das „Hochhaus von außen wie einen Wald maßloser Schatten erscheinen". Die Architekten vergleichen die ungewöhnliche Form des Hochhauses mit „einem belebten Wesen, das anscheinend nach unten auf die Landschaft schaut" und sich an der Basis verneigt, „um Passanten Platz zu machen".

Pour les architectes : « La tour Woermann incarne les illusions, les désirs et les rêves d'une société à la recherche d'un compromis entre la nature et le développement, d'une forme de vie intense fidèle au paysage : une autre beauté. » En dehors d'une place publique, le programme établi pour ce site central sensible comprenait des logements, des bureaux, des parkings, des commerces et une bibliothèque. La place pavée de pierre du Portugal a été conçue en collaboration avec l'artiste Albert Oehlen. Le bloc de sept niveaux qui s'élève au sud contient des bureaux et des commerces, tandis que la tour de 18 niveaux et 60 mètres de haut au nord est consacrée à la bibliothèque pour ses trois premiers niveaux et aux appartements pour les autres. Ceux-ci – quatre à cinq par étage – comptent de deux à cinq pièces. Les trois mètres qui séparent les niveaux permettent des proportions généreuses. Les façades de verre sont protégées du soleil par un système de brise-soleil et de motifs végétaux sablés dans le verre qui font que la « tour vue de l'extérieur donne l'impression d'une forêt d'ombres sans échelle ». Les architectes comparent la forme originale de cette tour à « un être animé inclinant la tête pour contempler le paysage, et qui se baisserait pour accueillir les piétons ».

The unusual top of the building makes it readily identifiable from a distance (right). The louvered exterior surfaces provide sun protection and give a distinctive appearance to the structure.

Dank seines ungewöhnlichen Aufbaus ist das Gebäude auch aus der Ferne leicht erkennbar (rechts). Die durch Jalousien vor Sonneneinstrahlung geschützten Außenflächen verleihen dem Bau ein prägnantes Aussehen.

L'étrange aspect du sommet de la tour lui permet d'être repérée de loin (à droite). L'enveloppe extérieure de pare-soleil qui protège de la lumière confère à l'ensemble un aspect particulier.

A section shows the connection below grade of the elements of the project, as well as the central square between the two blocks.

Der Schnitt zeigt sowohl die unterirdische Verbindung zwischen den Elementen des Projekts als auch den zentralen Platz zwischen den beiden Baublöcken.

Coupe montrant la connexion entre les parties du projet en sous-sol et la place centrale située entre les deux blocs.

Oficinas
Torre Residencial
Biblioteca
Oficinas Administración Local
Local Comercial
Aparcamiento Oficinas
Aparcamiento Torre Residencial
Instalaciónes

Vegetal window patterns at the ground level reinforce the architects' concept of a living structure, introduced by such other factors as the "movement" at the top of the building and its greenish colors.

Vegetabile Muster auf den Fenstern im Erdgeschoss unterstreichen die Idee der Architekten von einem lebendigen Bauwerk, unterstützt durch Elemente wie die „bewegte" Gebäudespitze und die grünlichen Farbtöne.

Des motifs végétaux sur les vitrages des ouvertures du rez-de-chaussée renforcent l'idée de structure vivante voulue par l'architecte, que viennent confirmer des éléments comme le « mouvement » en partie haute de la tour et les différentes nuances de vert de la façade.

Floor-to-ceiling windows offer generous, unobstructed ocean views. Leaning columns are a result of the unusual "nodding" top of the residential tower.

Deckenhohe Fenster bieten großzügige, ungehinderte Ausblicke auf das Meer. Geneigte Stützen sind die Folge der ungewöhnlichen „nickenden Spitze" des Wohnturms.

Des fenêtres toute hauteur ouvrent sur d'amples perspectives vers l'océan. L'inclinaison des colonnes s'explique par le « geste » qui anime le sommet de cette tour résidentielle.

#2

EDUARDO ARROYO

EDUARDO ARROYO
NO.MAD ARQUITECTOS, S. L.
c/ del Pez, 27, 1º izda.
28004 Madrid

Tel/Fax: +34 91 532 70 34
e-mail: nomad@nomad.as
Web: www.nomad.as

EDUARDO ARROYO was born in 1964 in Bilbao and graduated from the Escuela Técnica Superior de Arquitectura in Madrid (ETSAM) in 1988. He was a professor in the same school from 1996 to 2002. He has also taught in universities in Seoul, Teheran, Paris, Lausanne, Eindhoven, Graz, Ferrara, Porto, Lisbon, Oslo, Brussels, Buenos Aires, Barcelona, Alicante, Valencia, and Seville. As well as the two projects published here, his work includes: Children's School, Sondika (1997); El Desierto Square, Barakaldo (2000); and the Paris Olympic Villa competition entry (2000). More recent work includes: Euskotren Headquarters, Durango (competition entry 2003); Visitors Center and Elica Hotel, Fabriano, Italy (2003); Kaleido Restaurant, Madrid (2004); Musée des Beaux-Arts, Lausanne, Switzerland (NMBA, competition entry 2004); Estonian National Museum, Tartu, Estonia (competition entry 2005). He has also worked on urban design at the access and plaza for Etxebarria Park, Bilbao (2005). Current work includes: Social Housing for IVVSA, Valencia (2007–); Social Housing for EMVS, Madrid (2007–); Housing Tower, Durango (2007–); Housing and Sport Center, Valencia (2007–).

LASESARRE FOOTBALL STADIUM
BARAKALDO
1999 - 2003

CLIENT: Bilbao Ria 2000
AREA: 9260 m²
SITE AREA: 28.700 m²
COST: €10 million
COLLABORATORS: Nerea Calvillo,
Sergio L. Piñeiro, Héctor Mejia, Francesco Monaco,
Raul Ortega, Santiago Mazorriaga, Luis Arroyo

"How difficult it is to construct with nature," says Eduardo Arroyo. "It has always confronted us, and we only have coarse, limited resources to imitate it." In this instance, the architect used an "artificial/plant matter made of steel, vibrant beneath the folds of the awnings. The entrances through this fictitious green curtain bear us into a different geography that controls spectator flow and occupancy." The forms of the stadium are intended to resemble multiple buildings and indeed the volumes are intended to function separately if necessary. The Lasesarre Football Stadium is in fact used for various activities other than the stated function. The various "buildings" forming the structure are united by a strong roof. In typically poetic terms, the architect writes that at sunset, the "folded, translucent volume of the building turns into a soft origami-like lamp, capable of marking out a new luminous topography in its role as the emblem of the survival of an irrecoverable glorious past." The stadium sits on 40-meter-deep piles "to escape from the polluted sludge that embraces the Nervion River estuary." For all this hidden mass of steel, what strikes visitors entering the stadium when it is still mostly empty, is the surprising variety of colors of the seats: "But here they go," says Arroyo, "all mixed up, like the population itself."

„Wie schwierig es doch ist, mit der Natur zu bauen", sagt Eduardo Arroyo. „Wir waren immer mit ihr konfrontiert und wir verfügen nur über grobe, begrenzte Mittel, um sie nachzuahmen." In diesem Fall verwendete der Architekt ein „künstlich/pflanzliches Material aus Stahl, das unter den Falten des Sonnenschutzes vibriert. Die Zugänge durch diesen fiktiven grünen Vorhang tragen uns in eine andere Geografie, die die hereinströmenden Zuschauer zu ihren Plätzen lenkt." Die Formen des Stadions sollen mehrere eigenständige Bauten vortäuschen und tatsächlich können die Bauteile wenn nötig separat genutzt werden. Über seine Funktion als Austragungsort für Fußballspiele hinaus kann das Lasesarre-Stadion für vielfältige andere Aktivitäten genutzt werden. Die verschiedenen Teile, aus denen sich das Stadion zusammensetzt, werden durch eine ausdrucksstarke Dachform geeint. In typisch poetischer Sprache schreiben die Architekten, dass sich bei untergehender Sonne „der gefaltete, durchscheinende Baukörper in eine matte, origamiartige Lampe verwandelt, fähig, eine neue leuchtende Topografie zu markieren in seiner Rolle als Emblem des Nachlebens einer unwiederbringlichen ruhmreichen Vergangenheit". Das Stadion steht auf 40 m tiefen Gründungspfählen, „um dem verseuchten Schlick zu entgehen, der die Flussmündung des Nervion bedeckt". Ungeachtet dieser verborgenen Masse von Stahl fällt Besuchern, die das noch weitgehend leere Stadion betreten, v. a. die überraschende farbige Vielfalt der Sitzplätze auf - „aber bitte", sagt Arroyo, „gründlich gemischt, genau wie die Bevölkerung".

« Qu'il est difficile de construire à partir de la nature... », affirme Eduardo Arroyo. « Nous y sommes toujours confrontés et nous ne disposons que de ressources limitées pour l'imiter », poursuit-il. À Barakaldo, l'architecte a fait appel à un « matériau naturel / artificiel en acier, qui vibre en sous-face des auvents. Les entrées qui permettent de traverser ce rideau vert de fiction nous transportent dans une géographie différente qui contrôle les flux et la répartition des spectateurs. » Les formes du stade évoquent un assemblage de plusieurs constructions et les volumes peuvent fonctionner séparément si nécessaire. Le stade est destiné à de multiples activités qui peuvent ne pas être sportives. Les différents « bâtiments » constituant la structure sont assemblés par une toiture au dessin plein de force. À sa façon poétique caractéristique, l'architecte écrit : « Au coucher du soleil, le volume plié et translucide du bâtiment se transforme en une sorte de lampe en origami capable de créer une nouvelle topographie lumineuse, à l'image de la survie d'un passé à jamais glorieux. » Le stade repose sur des pieux de 40 mètres de profondeur « pour dépasser le terrain bourbeux et pollué qui occupe l'estuaire du Nervion ». En dehors de cette masse d'acier, ce qui frappe les visiteurs pénétrant dans le stade lorsqu'il est encore presque vide est la surprenante variété des couleurs des sièges. « Tout est mêlé, comme la population elle-même », commente Arroyo.

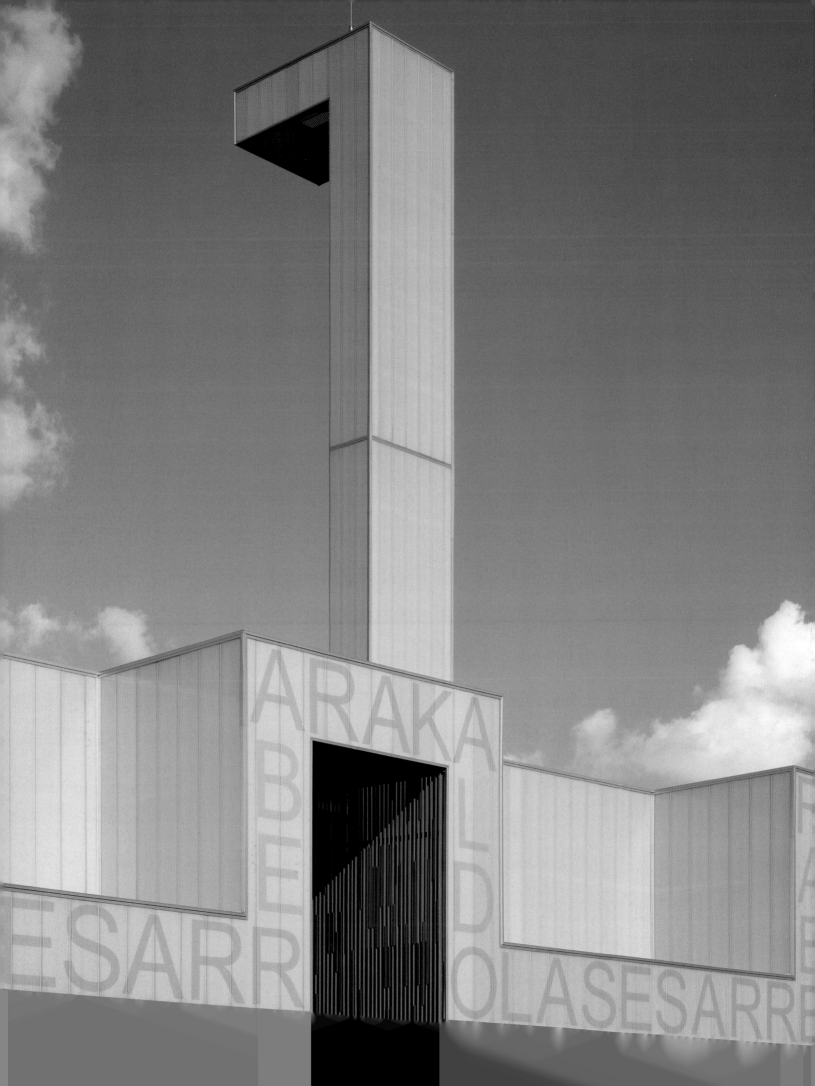

The sharp geometric and largely horizontal lines of the stadium contrast with the more frequent bowl-like design of most other facilities of this nature. Surface treatments (left) also give the stadium an unexpected appearance.

Die präzisen geometrischen und überwiegend horizontalen Linien des Stadions stehen in Kontrast zur schüsselartigen Form der meisten anderen Bauten dieser Art. Darüber hinaus lassen die strukturierten Oberflächen (links) das Bauwerk ungewöhnlich aussehen.

L'orthogonalité appuyée et l'horizontalité des lignes d'ensemble contrastent avec les plans en forme de coupe fréquemment utilisés pour ce type d'équipement. Le traitement de certaines surfaces (à gauche) donne également au stade un aspect surprenant.

The colored seats of the stadium animate its interior, even when it is empty. The overhangs provide shelter from rain or sun to some extent as well as lighting.

Die bunten Sitzflächen des Stadions beleben den Innenraum, selbst wenn er leer ist. Die Überstände bieten Schutz vor Regen oder Sonne wie auch Beleuchtung.

Les sièges colorés animent les gradins même lorsque le stade est vide. Le porte-à-faux protège de la pluie ou du soleil, et régule l'éclairage naturel.

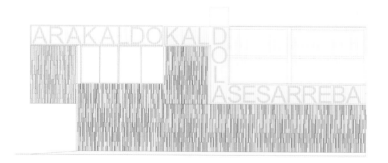

The snaking, geometric exterior band of the stadium is lit in a continuous pattern, making the structure readily identifiable.

Das mäandrierende äußere Band des Stadions ist in einem fortlaufenden Muster beleuchtet und macht das Bauwerk leicht erkennbar.

Le bandeau extérieur géométrique ondulé s'éclaire en dessinant un motif continu qui renforce l'identité du projet.

LEVENE HOUSE
SAN LORENZO DE EL ESCORIAL
2002 · 05

CLIENT: Richard Levene
AREA: 400 m²
COST: €1 200 000
COLLABORATORS: Francesco Monaco,
Javier Tamer Elshiekh, Cristina Fidalgo

In a somewhat polemical vein, Eduardo Arroyo writes, "For the concept of this home, we asked ourselves whether we were capable of building something while maintaining the utmost respect for the natural surroundings, avoiding speaking about sustainability, alternative energy or ecology as a veneer for modernity and political correctness." The volume of the house was thus adapted to the trees on the site and to the topography of the land. The "non-Cartesian" geometry used for the architecture is thus intimately related to the surroundings. Arroyo divided the general volume into what he calls "specialized fingers" or specific programmatic elements. Two of these fingers are intended for family rooms, another for an indoor pool, another for a kitchen-dining room and so forth. The entrance from the highest level leads down to the lowest space, the master bedroom, a gym and sauna. Openings in the façades of the house were also determined by the specific presence of trees. The density of the glazing, transparent, etched, or translucent, depends on the type of light in each space, thus affirming "the influence of the forest on this strange object that has invaded the tranquility of its territory." Amber resin with wooden slats is used for floors, walls or ceilings. "A strange feature," concludes Arroyo, "slides along the upper floors, a reflection of the owner's collector behavior. Its polycarbonate structure with iridescent sheens holds a mass of tiny inhabitants whose presence filters the boring collective exterior in a personal, non-transferable interior." These tiny inhabitants are the owner's collection of Action Man toy figures.

Etwas polemisch schreibt Eduardo Arroyo: „Bei der Konzeption dieses Hauses fragten wir uns, ob wir in der Lage sein würden, etwas zu bauen und dabei den größtmöglichen Respekt für die umgebende Natur zu bewahren; außerdem wollten wir die Erwähnung von Nachhaltigkeit, alternativer Energie oder Ökologie als Fassade für Modernität und „political correctness' vermeiden." Also wurde die Größe des Hauses den vorhandenen Bäumen und der Topografie des Geländes angepasst. Die für die Architektur verwendete „nicht-kartesianische" Geometrie ist folglich eng auf die Umgebung bezogen. Arroyo unterteilte den Baukörper in, wie er das nennt, „spezialisierte Finger" oder spezifische programmatische Elemente. Zwei dieser Finger sind für Wohnräume vorgesehen, ein anderer für ein Schwimmbecken, ein weiterer für eine Kombination aus Küche und Esszimmer usw. Vom Eingang auf der obersten Ebene gelangt man hinunter zu den tiefliegendsten Räumlichkeiten, dem Elternschlafzimmer, einem Fitnessraum und der Sauna. Auch die Öffnungen in der Fassade wurden von der Präsenz besonderer Bäume be-

stimmt. Von der Dichte des Glases, ob klar, geätzt oder halb durchscheinend, hängt die Art des Lichts in jedem Raum ab und bestätigt „den Einfluss des Waldes auf dieses fremdartige Objekt, das in die Stille seines Hoheitsgebiets eingedrungen ist". Bernsteinfarbenes Harz und Holzbohlen wurden für Böden, Wände und Decken verwendet. „Eine Besonderheit", berichtet Arroyo abschließend, „bewegt sich entlang der Obergeschosse und ist Ausdruck der Sammlertätigkeit des Eigentümers. Die Struktur aus Polycarbonat mit irisierendem Glanz enthält eine große Menge winziger Bewohner, deren Präsenz das langweilige Äußere insgesamt in ein individuelles, nicht übertragbares Interieur filtert." Bei diesen Bewohnern handelt es sich um des Hauherrn Sammlung von Action-Man-Spielzeugfiguren.

Sur un mode légèrement polémique, Eduardo Arroyo écrit : « Pour le concept de cette maison, nous nous sommes demandés si nous étions capables de construire quelque chose qui respecterait le plus possible l'environnement naturel, sans pour autant parler de développement durable, d'énergies alternatives ou d'écologie, ces « placages » de modernité et du politiquement correct. » Le volume de la maison a ainsi été adapté à la présence des arbres sur le site et à la topographie. Sa géométrie « non cartésienne » est donc intimement liée à l'environnement. Arroyo a divisé le grand volume en ce qu'il appelle « des doigts spécialisés » ou composants programmatiques spécifiques. Deux de ces « doigts » sont destinés aux pièces de séjour familiales, un autre à une piscine intérieure, un a une cuisine-salle à manger, etc. De l'entrée, à laquelle on accède par le niveau supérieur, on descend vers les pièces situées plus bas, la chambre principale, une salle de gymnastique et un sauna. Les ouvertures en façade sont également déterminées par la présence spécifique des arbres. La densité du vitrage, transparent, sablé ou translucide dépend du type de lumière nécessaire à chaque volume intérieur, confirmant « l'influence de la forêt sur cet étrange objet qui a bousculé la tranquillité de son territoire ». Les sols, les murs et les plafonds sont recouverts d'une résine de couleur ambrée et de lattes de bois. « Un élément étrange, conclut Arroyo, se glisse le long des niveaux supérieurs et illustre le comportement de collectionneur du propriétaire. Cette structure en polycarbonate aux luisances iridescentes contient une masse de petits habitants dont la présence tempère l'aspect répétitif de son ennuyeux contenant en lui octroyant un intérieur singulier que personne d'autre ne pourrait s'attribuer. » Ces « petits habitants » sont une collection de poupées-jouets Action-Man du propriétaire.

Extensive terraces and openings characterize the house, but despite the multifaceted design there is a continuity and coherence in the architecture.

Großzügige Terrassen und Öffnungen kennzeichnen das Haus, dessen Architektur sich ungeachtet ihres facettenreichen Charakters durch Kontinuität und Kohärenz auszeichnet.

De vastes terrasses et ouvertures caractérisent cette maison dont le plan à multiples facettes ne contredit pas la continuité et la cohérence architecturales.

The unusually complex plan of the house allows it to fit into its natural setting with minimum damage to the existing trees. The use of ample glazed surfaces reinforces the connection of the residence to its natural setting.

Der ungewöhnlich komplexe Grundriss des Hauses fügt sich bei minimaler Beeinträchtigung der vorhandenen Bäume in die umgebende Natur ein. Die großzügige Durchfensterung der Wände akzentuiert die Verbindung des Wohnhauses zu seiner Umgebung.

Le plan inhabituellement complexe de cette maison lui permet de s'intégrer dans son cadre tout en portant le minimum d'atteinte aux arbres existants. Les vastes surfaces vitrées renforcent le lien entre la résidence et son environnement naturel.

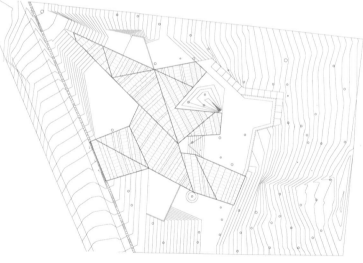

As the sections below demonstrate, the house rises and falls in response to the topography of the site. Glazed angles rise against the forest backdrop (above) making the Levene House appear to be a part of its setting, rather than an alien element.

Wie auf dem Schnitt unten zu sehen, steigt und fällt das Haus entsprechend der Topografie des Grundstücks. Vor dem dahinter liegenden Wald erheben sich verglaste Ecken (oben), die die Casa Levene als Teil der Umgebung und nicht als Fremdkörper erscheinen lassen.

Comme le montre la coupe ci-dessous, les contours de la maison s'abaissent et s'élèvent en fonction de la topographie. Des pans inclinés vitrés se dressent face à la forêt (ci-dessus). Ils ont pour effet d'intégrer la maison à son site qui n'apparaît plus alors comme un corps étranger.

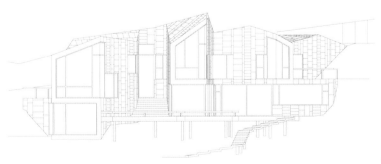

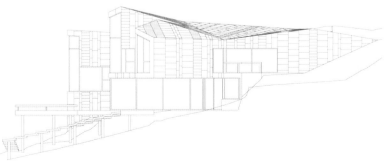

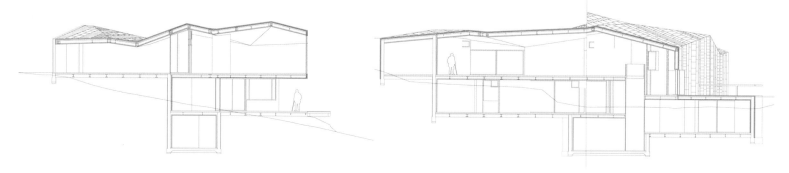

The different levels of the house are not continuous but vary as the land allows. Rather than imposing an artificial regularity on the site, the architect has preferred to move with the topography.

Die verschiedenen Ebenen des Hauses sind nicht durchgehend, sondern variieren gemäß dem Terrain. Anstatt dem Baugrund eine künstliche Regelmäßigkeit aufzupropfen, vollzog der Architekt lieber die topografischen Gegebenheiten nach.

Les différents niveaux de la maison ne sont pas continus, mais s'adaptent au profil du terrain. Plutôt que d'imposer un ordre artificiel, l'architecte a préféré suivre la topographie.

The complex articulation of the plan of the house is echoed in such interior views as the one to the right, where the surface planes are varied through the use of lighting, glazing, or opaque surfaces.

Die Komplexität des Entwurfs spiegelt sich in Innenansichten wie der rechts, wo die Beschaffenheit der Flächen sich durch den Einsatz von Licht, Verglasung oder opaken Materialien unterscheidet.

L'articulation complexe du plan de la maison se retrouve en écho dans ces vues intérieures (notamment celle de droite), dans lesquelles les surfaces varient en fonction de l'éclairage, de la transparence ou de l'opacité des plans.

The sense of movement visible in the exterior of the house is very much a part of its interior, where shifting wall surfaces and varied glazing patterns bring light in and diffuse it in constantly changing ways.

Der im Äußeren des Hauses wahrnehmbare Eindruck von Bewegung prägt erst recht das Innere, wo verschiebbare Wandflächen und unterschiedliche Glasmusterungen Licht in ständig wechselnder Weise einfallen lassen oder streuen.

Le sentiment de mouvement tangible à l'extérieur de la maison se retrouve à l'intérieur où des surfaces filantes et divers types de vitrages apportent la lumière et la diffusent de manière constamment changeante.

SANTIAGO CALATRAVA

SANTIAGO CALATRAVA S. A.
Parkring 11
8002 Zurich

Tel: +41 1 20 45 00 0
Fax: +41 1 20 45 00 1
e-mail: admin.zurich@calatrava.com
Web: www.calatrava.com

Born in Valencia in 1951, **SANTIAGO CALATRAVA** studied art and architecture at the Escuela Técnica Superior de Arquitectura in Valencia (1968–73) and engineering at the ETH in Zurich (doctorate in Technical Science, 1981). He opened his own architecture and civil engineering office the same year. His built work includes the Bach de Roda-Felipe II Bridge, Barcelona (1984–87); the Gallery and Heritage Square, BCE Place Toronto, Canada (1987–92); the Montjuic Tower, Barcelona (1989–92); the Lyon Satolas TGV Station (1989–94); and the Kuwait Pavilion at Expo '92, Seville, and the Alamillo Bridge for the same exhibition. He completed the Oriente Station in Lisbon in 1998. He recently completed the Sondica Airport, Bilbao (1990–2000); and the Pont de l'Europe in Orléans, France (1996–2000). Other recent work includes: James Joyce Bridge, Dublin, Ireland (2003); Tenerife Auditorium Santa Cruz de Tenerife (1991–2003); Milwaukee Art Museum, Milwaukee (1994–2001); the Valencia Opera House (1996–2006); Sundial Bridge, Redding California (1995–2004); Petah-Tikva Bridge, Tel Aviv, Israel (1998–2006); and the Athens Olympic Sports Complex, Greece (2001–04). He is currently working on the World Trade Center Transportation Hub in New York; the Liege-Guillemins TGV Railway Station, Liege, Belgium (1996–); Reggio Emilia Bridges and Train Station, Reggio Emilia, Italy (2002–); Atlanta Symphony Orchestra Hall, Atlanta, Georgia (2002–); Valencia Towers, Valencia, Spain (2004–); Universita degli Studi di Roma Tor Vergata, Città della Sport, Rome, Italy (2005–); Chicago Spire, Chicago, Illinois, United States (2005–); and the Palacio de Congresos Princesa Letizia, Oviedo, Spain (2005–). Santiago Calatrava received the American Institute of Architects (AIA) 2005 Gold Medal.

TENERIFE AUDITORIUM
SANTA CRUZ DE TENERIFE 1991 - 2003

CLIENT: Tenerife Town Council
BUILDING AREA: 17 270 m²
COST: €65 700 000
CAPACITY: 1558 persons (main concert hall);
428 persons (chamber music hall)

Completed in 2003, this 1558-seat capacity concert hall is located at the intersection of the Tres de Mayo Avenue and Maritima Avenue in the city of Santa Cruz de Tenerife. The facility also includes a chamber music hall with seating for 428. On this site in the harbor, the city expressed "a desire for a dynamic, monumental building that would not only be a place for music and culture but would also create a focal point for the area." With its distinctive concrete shell roof, in a curved triangular form culminating 60 meters above the plaza surrounding the building, this concert hall is one of the most visually spectacular structures designed by Calatrava. Beyond the basic functions of the project, it clearly takes on a symbolic value by the very nature of its appearance. Located on a 154 x 100 meter rectangular site that has the particularity of including a 60-meter change in levels, the concert hall is set on a stepped platform or plinth that contains technical facilities and changing rooms. As the architect says of the actual concert space, "To fine-tune the acoustics, the wood paneling of the interior takes on a crystalline form, which also contributes to the drama of the space. These fittings were determined by investigations on models at 1:10. The placing of sound reflectors was determined by laser tests, which also helped define the dimensions of the vaulted interior. Instead of having stage curtains, the auditorium is provided with a concertina screen of vertical aluminum slats, which upon opening lift up into the auditorium to act as a sound-reflector above the orchestra pit." The roof of the shell of the structure is clad in broken tile, while local volcanic basalt is used for much of the paving and the cladding of the plinth. A 50-meter-high dome covers the main hall, recalling a number of Santiago Calatrava's studies of the human eye and its lid.

Diese 2003 fertig gestellte Konzerthalle mit 1558 Sitzplätzen steht an der Kreuzung der Avenida Tres de Mayo mit der Avenida Maritima in der Stadt Santa Cruz de Tenerife. Der Bau umfasst außerdem einen Kammermusiksaal mit 428 Plätzen. An dieser Stelle des Hafens wünschte sich die Stadt „ein dynamisches, monumentales Bauwerk, das nicht nur ein Ort für Musik und Kultur sein sollte, sondern auch ein Wahrzeichen für die Gegend". Mit ihrem charakteristischen Betonschalendach, das sich in gebogener Dreiecksform 60 m über die das Gebäude umgebende Plaza aufschwingt, stellt die Konzerthalle einen der in visueller Hinsicht ungewöhnlichsten Bauten Calatravas dar. Über seine Funktionalität hinaus erhält das Projekt allein durch sein Aussehen eine symbolische Wertigkeit. Das 154 x 100 m große rechteckige Gelände der Konzerthalle weist einen Höhenunterschied von 60 m auf. Die Halle selbst wurde auf einem abgetreppten Sockel errichtet, in dem technische Einrichtungen und Umkleideräume untergebracht sind. Zum eigentlichen Konzertraum sagt der Architekt: „Um die Akustik genau abzustimmen, erhielt die Holzverkleidung des Innenraums eine kristalline Formgebung, die außerdem zur Dramatik des Raumes beiträgt. Über diese Einbauten wurde nach Versuchen mit einem Modell im Maßstab 1:10 entschieden. Die Platzierung von Klangreflektoren wurde durch Lasertests bestimmt, die auch halfen, die Abmessungen des gewölbten Innenraums festzulegen. Anstelle von Bühnenvorhängen ist das Auditorium mit einem Ziehharmonikaschirm aus vertikalen Aluminiumlamellen ausgerüstet, der sich beim Öffnen in das Auditorium hinein erhebt und über dem Orchestergraben als Klangreflektor fungiert." Die Decke der Schalenkonstruktion des Gebäudes ist mit Kachelscherben ausgekleidet, während für einen Großteil der Pflasterung und die Sockelverkleidung heimischer, vulkanischer Basalt verwendet wurde. Der Hauptsaal ist von einer 50 m hohen Kuppel überwölbt, die an einige Studien Calatravas zum menschlichen Auge und Augenlid erinnert.

Achevé en 2003, ce complexe qui comprend une salle de concert symphonique de 1558 places et une salle destinée à la musique de chambre de 428 places est situé à l'intersection de l'avenue Tres de Mayo et de l'avenue Maritima à Santa Cruz de Tenerife. Pour ce terrain en bordure du port, la ville avait exprimé « le désir d'un bâtiment monumental et dynamique qui devienne non seulement un lieu consacré à la musique et à la culture, mais également un pôle d'attraction pour l'ensemble de cette zone ». Avec son toit extrêmement original, fait d'une coque de béton triangulaire incurvée culminant à 60 mètres au-dessus d'une place, cette salle est l'un des projets les plus spectaculaires de Calatrava. Sa valeur symbolique et la nature même de sa présence prennent le pas sur ses fonctions de base. Édifiée sur un terrain rectangulaire de 154 x 100 mètres marqué par une différence de niveaux de 60 mètres, la salle est posée sur une plate-forme en gradins, ou plinthes, qui contient les équipements techniques et les loges pour artistes. Calatrava explique ainsi l'aménagement intérieur de la salle : « C'est pour affiner l'acoustique que nous avons donné au lambrissage en bois à l'intérieur l'apparence cristalline qui contribue à l'aspect spectaculaire du volume. Ces installations ont été mises au point grâce à des études menées sur maquettes au 1/10e. Le placement des réflecteurs sonores a été déterminé à l'aide de tests au laser qui ont également permis de définir les dimensions du volume intérieur voûté. À la place du classique rideau de scène, l'auditorium est équipé d'un écran de lattes d'aluminium verticales qui s'élève dans les cintres et sert de réflecteur sonore une fois replié au-dessus de l'orchestre. » La couverture de la coque est en carrelage brisé et un basalte local a été choisi pour la plus grande partie des sols et de l'habillage de la plinthe. La coupole de 50 mètres de haut, qui recouvre la salle principale, rappelle un certain nombre d'études de Santiago Calatrava sur l'œil et la paupière.

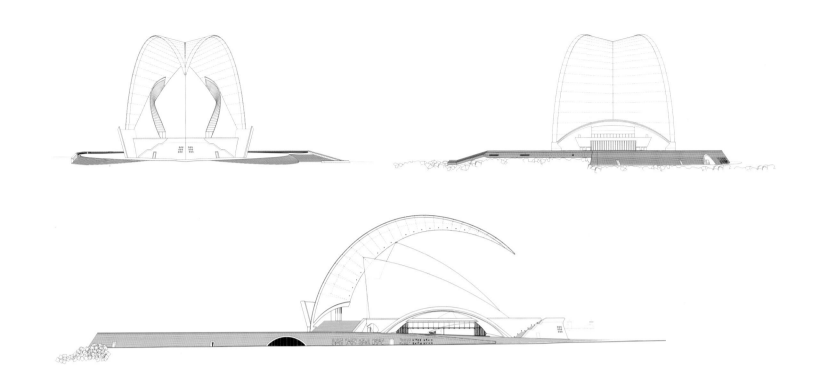

Many of Santiago Calatrava's favored images are present in this design, including his frequent reference to the (architect's) eye. The silhouette of the building is nothing if not distinctive.

Viele von Santiago Calatravas bevorzugten Bildern sind in diesem Entwurf präsent, so auch sein häufiger Verweis auf das Auge (des Architekten). Der Umriss des Gebäudes ist äußerst markant.

Beaucoup d'images qui ont la faveur de Calatrava sont reprises dans ce projet, y compris sa fréquente référence à l'œil (de l'architecte). La silhouette de ce bâtiment est totalement originale.

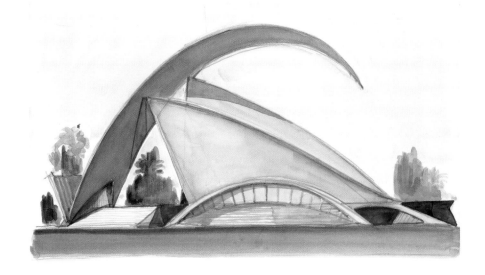

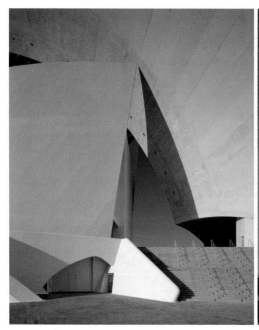  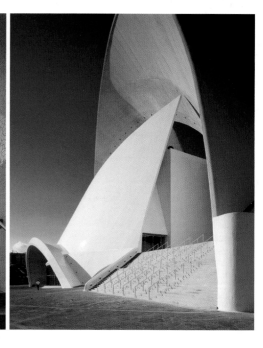

The interior of the building offers a marked continuity with the exterior, and a variety of spaces sometimes bordering on an almost surreal complexity.

Das Gebäudeinnere stellt eine deutliche Fortsetzung des Außenbaus dar und bietet eine bisweilen an nahezu surreale Komplexität grenzende Vielzahl von Räumen.

L'intérieur de l'immeuble présente une continuité marquée avec l'extérieur. Divers espaces sont d'une complexité quasi-irréelle.

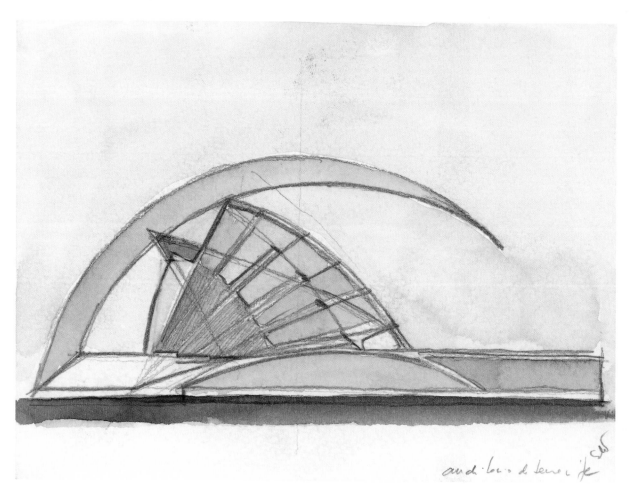

The curves and angles of the overall design find spectacular echoes in the interior. Rather than simply creating an efficient envelope for an auditorium, the architect has set out to create a spatial experience.

Kurven und Schrägen des Gesamtentwurfs finden einen spektakulären Niederschlag im Inneren. Anstatt einer bloßen Hülle für ein Auditorium wollte der Architekt eine räumliche Erfahrung schaffen.

Les courbes et les inclinaisons du plan général se retrouvent en écho à l'intérieur. Plutôt que de se contenter de créer une enveloppe efficace, l'architecte a cherché à susciter une expérience spatiale.

The architect's sketches reveal the precise iterations and development of the overall forms, sometimes approaching the image of the human eye, but steering clear of any specific anthropomorphic elements.

Die Skizzen des Architekten offenbaren die schrittweise Annäherung und die Entwicklung der Gesamtformen, die sich gelegentlich dem Bild des menschlichen Auges nähern, spezifisch anthropomorphe Elemente jedoch vermeiden.

Les croquis de l'architecte montrent les répétitions et le développement des formes, se rapprochant parfois d'une représentation d'œil humain, mais sans tomber pour autant dans un anthropomorphisme précis.

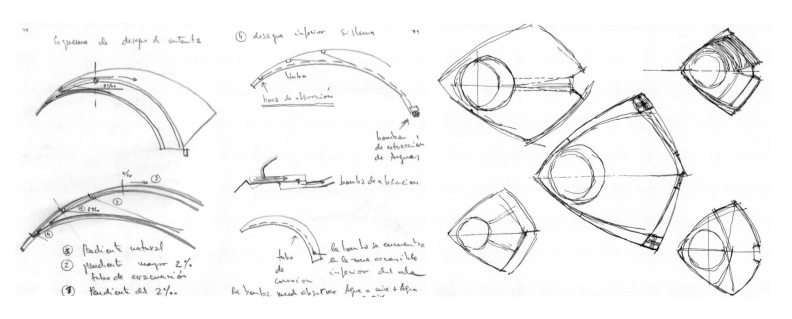

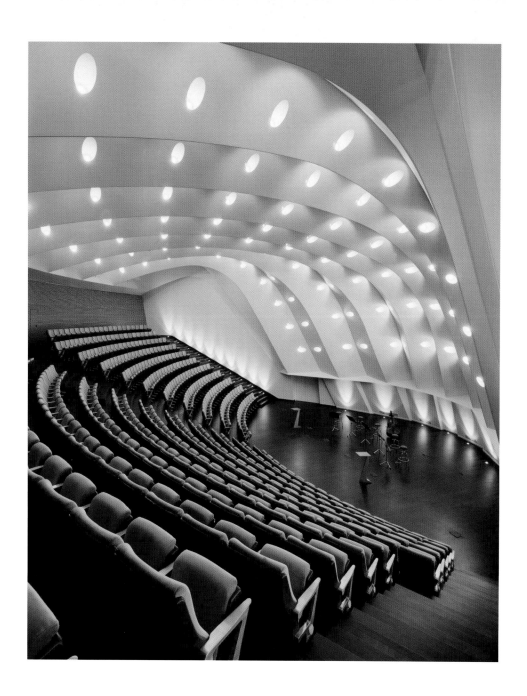

A plan shows the precise division of the building with its two curving theaters. The acoustic ceiling to the right, with its sunburst pattern, brings the drama of the auditorium's exterior into the functional space of the building.

Ein Grundriss zeigt die genaue Unterteilung des Gebäudes mit den beiden geschwungenen Theatersälen. Die akustische Decke rechts mit dem Motiv der Sonne transponiert das dramatische Äußere des Auditoriums in den funktionalen Innenraum.

Plan montrant l'organisation du bâtiment et de ses deux salles. Le plafond acoustique (à droite), en motif de lever de soleil, cite un élément naturel extérieur spectaculaire à l'intérieur du volume fonctionnel du bâtiment.

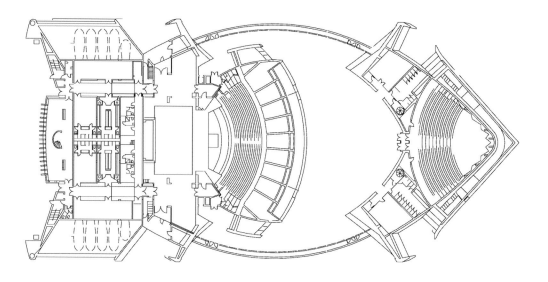

VALENCIA OPERA HOUSE
VALENCIA
1996 - 2006

CLIENT: Autonomous Government of
Valencia, City of Arts and Science S. A.
TOTAL BUILDING AREA: 44 100 m²
SITE AREA: Opera House: 3.3 hectares

Conceived as the largest element in the City of Arts and Sciences complex, rising to a height of 75 meters on its western edge, the Valencia Opera House was "designed as a series of apparently random volumes, which become unified through their enclosure within two symmetrical, cut-away concrete shells. These forms are crowned by a steel sheath, which projects axially from the entrance concourse out over the uppermost contours of the curvilinear envelope. The structure that results defines the identity of the Opera House, enhancing its symbolic and dynamic effect within the landscape, while offering protection to the terraces and facilities beneath." Calatrava defines the design as being akin to a "monumental sculpture." The central volume of the complex is occupied by the 1706-seat auditorium as well as the equipment required for the stage settings. A smaller auditorium, conceived mainly for chamber music, seats 380, while a large auditorium to the east, partially covered by the open shell, can seat 1520 persons. The first concert was held on October 8, 2005, but the opera house was actually completed late in 2006. The architect created two large murals for the main auditorium and restaurant and two low-relief sculptures. The five structures of the complex are linked by gardens and bodies of water.

Als größtes Element der Stadt der Künste und Wissenschaft konzipiert, entstand das am Westrand der Anlage erbaute, 75 m hohe Opernhaus als „Reihe scheinbar zufälliger Baukörper, die durch zwei symmetrische, ausgeschnittene Betonschalen zusammengeschlossen werden. Diese Formen werden von einer stählernen Scheide bekrönt, die vom Eingangsvorplatz in axialer Richtung über den höchsten Punkt der gebogenen Umhüllung reicht. Dieses Element bestimmt die Identität des Opernhauses und steigert seine symbolische und dynamische Wirkung in der Landschaft, während es gleichzeitig den Terrassen und darunterliegenden Einrichtungen Schutz bietet." Calatrava zufolge ähnelt dieser Entwurf einer „monumentalen Skulptur". Der zentrale Raum des Komplexes enthält das Auditorium mit 1706 Sitzplätzen sowie die für die Bühnenbilder erforderlichen Vorrichtungen. Ein in erster Linie für Kammermusik vorgesehenes Auditorium bietet 380 Plätze, während in einer größeren, nach Osten gelegenen Halle 1520 Personen Platz finden; sie ist teilweise von der offenen Betonschale überdeckt. Das erste Konzert fand am 8. Oktober 2005 statt, aber das Opernhaus wurde erst Ende 2006 vollständig fertig gestellt. Für den Hauptsaal und das Restaurant schuf der Architekt zwei großflächige Wandbilder sowie zwei Reliefs. Zwischen den fünf Baukörpern des Komplexes befinden sich verbindende Grünanlagen und Wasserflächen.

Plus grand élément du complexe de la Cité des arts et des sciences de Valence et s'élevant à l'ouest de celui-ci a une hauteur de 75 mètres, cet opéra a été « conçu comme une série de volumes apparemment aléatoires, unifiés par leur clôture, deux coques en béton symétriques et découpées. Celles-ci sont couronnées par un couvercle-auvent d'acier projeté à partir de l'axe du hall d'entrée et dépassant la hauteur de l'enveloppe curviligne de béton. Le profil qui en résulte définit l'identité de cet opéra par la mise en exergue dans le paysage de sa dynamique et de sa symbolique, tout en protégeant les terrasses et les installations situées en dessous ». Calatrava définit le projet comme proche d'une « sculpture monumentale ». Le volume central est occupé par la salle de 1706 places et les équipements de scène. On trouve par ailleurs une salle plus petite de 380 places, principalement prévue pour la musique de chambre, et, à l'est, un grand auditorium de 1520 places en partie protégé sous la coque ouverte. Le premier concert a été donné le 8 octobre 2005, mais l'opéra n'a été achevé que fin 2006. L'architecte créa deux grandes peintures murales ainsi que deux bas-reliefs pour la salle principale et le restaurant. Les cinq éléments qui composent le complexe de Valence sont reliés par des jardins et des bassins.

Part of a group of buildings on the same site designed by Calatrava, the Opera House has a typically distinctive profile, and a dynamic exterior shell that reveals inner surfaces in an almost organic manner.

Das Opernhaus, das Calatrava als Teil einer Gruppe von Bauten auf dem gleichen Gelände entwarf, zeichnet sich durch ein markantes Profil und eine dynamische äußere Hülle aus, die innere Oberflächen auf fast organische Weise offenlegt.

Faisant partie d'un ensemble de bâtiments édifiés par Calatrava, l'opéra présente un profil original et dynamique qui exprime ses volumes intérieurs de façon presque organique.

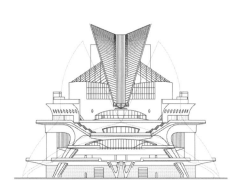
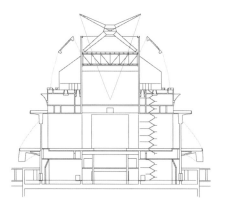
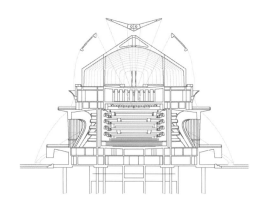

Below, a bridge designed by the architect-engineer is seen in front of the Opera House. Two sections show the means used to juxtapose dynamic, frequently cantilevered volumes inside the building, thus reflecting its exterior movement.

Unten ist die von Calatrava entworfene Brücke vor dem Opernhaus zu sehen. Zwei Schnitte zeigen, wie dynamische, häufig auskragende Räume im Inneren des Gebäudes nebeneinander angeordnet sind und somit die äußere Bewegung reflektieren.

Ci-dessous, un pont conçu par l'architecte-ingénieur devant l'opéra. Deux coupes montrent les moyens utilisés pour juxtaposer les volumes intérieurs dynamiques, souvent en porte-à-faux, qui expriment l'effet de mouvement qui se produit à l'extérieur.

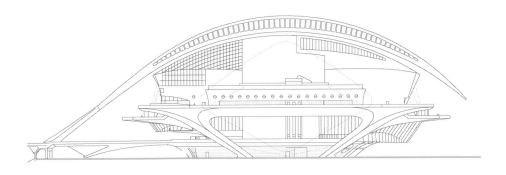

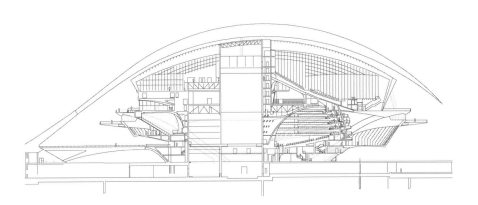

ALBERTO CAMPO BAEZA

ESTUDIO ALBERTO CAMPO BAEZA
c/ Almirante, 9, 2° izda.
28004 Madrid

Tel: +34 91 701 06 95
Fax: +34 91 521 70 61
e-mail: estudio@campobaeza.com
Web: www.campobaeza.com

Born in Valladolid in 1946, **ALBERTO CAMPO BAEZA** studied in Madrid where he obtained his Ph. D. in 1982 at the Escuela Técnica Superior de Arquitectura (ETSAM). He has taught in Madrid, at the ETH in Zürich (1989-90), at Cornell University, and at the University of Pennsylvania (1986 and 1999); and ETSAM where he has served as Head Professor of Design. His work includes the Fene Town Hall (1980); S. Fermín Public School, Madrid (1985); Public Library, Orihuela (1992); a Public School, Cádiz (1992); the BIT Center in Mallorca (1998); as well as a number of private houses, such as the Belvedere, De Blas House, Sevilla de la Nueva, Madrid (2000). In 2001 he completed what he considers his most representative building, the Caja General de Granada Headquarters. In 2002 he finished an office building for the Health Council of the Government of Andalucía in Almería, and the SM Editorial building in Madrid, and in 2005 the Guerrero House in Cádiz published here.

GUERRERO HOUSE
CÁDIZ
2004-05

AREA: 170 m² (house); 400 m² (patios)
COST: €240 404
COLLABORATORS: Ignacio Aguirre, Miguel Vela

Alberto Campo Baeza calls this the "House of Shadows." His goal was to "construct a house full of light and well-balanced shade. To create a luminous darkness." To attain this goal, he imagined walls no less than eight meters high. A central 9 x 9 meter patio, sheltered by these high walls, thus becomes a shaded space, despite the almost relentlessly bright skies of Cádiz. The external appearance of the house is almost abstract, like a blank white sculpture. This type of extreme minimalism is relatively typical of the work of Campo Baeza, but here it attains a purity and simplicity that is enriched by the movement of light. Front and back openings are protected by three-meter-deep porches with bedrooms and bathrooms on either side. Four cypresses mark the center and main axes of the front patio, while another four cypresses are aligned in the rear patio. A pond excavated in the earth marks the end of the house "from one end to the other."

Alberto Campo Baeza nennt diesen Bau das „Haus der Schatten". Sein Ziel war es, „ein Haus voller Licht und wohl ausgewogener Schattenzonen zu errichten, eine leuchtende Dunkelheit zu erschaffen." Um dieses Ziel zu erreichen, entwarf er bis zu 8 m hohe Wände. Der von diesen Mauern umgebene, zentrale, 9 x 9 m messende Patio wird so zu einem schattigen Raum, ungeachtet des anhaltend wolkenlosen Himmels über Cádiz. Das Äußere des Hauses wirkt nahezu abstrakt wie eine reinweiße Skulptur. Diese Form eines für das Werk Campo Baezas recht typischen, extremen Minimalismus führt in diesem Fall jedoch zu einer von Lichtbewegungen bereicherten großen Reinheit und Schlichtheit. Öffnungen auf der Vorder- und Rückseite werden durch 3 m tief eingeschnittene Windfänge geschützt, zu deren Seiten jeweils Schlafzimmer und Bäder liegen. Vier Zypressen markieren das Zentrum und die Hauptachse des vorderen Patios; auf dem rückseitigen Patio stehen vier weitere Zypressen in Reih und Glied. Ein aus dem Erdreich ausgehobenes Becken markiert das Ende des Hauses „von einer Seite zur anderen".

Alberto Campo Baeza évoque pour ce projet une « maison des ombres ». Son objectif était de « construire une maison pleine de lumière et d'ombres équilibrées pour créer une obscurité lumineuse ». Pour le réaliser, il a dessiné des murs de pas moins de huit mètres de haut. Le patio central de 9 x 9 mètres de surface, protégé par ces hauts murs, est devenu un lieu ombreux, malgré la luminosité implacable du ciel de Cadix. La forme extérieure de la maison, presque abstraite, fait penser à une sculpture blanche massive. Ce type de minimalisme extrême est relativement typique de l'œuvre de Campo Baeza, mais il atteint ici une pureté et une simplicité encore enrichies par le jeu de la lumière. Les ouvertures vers l'avant et vers l'arrière sont protégées par des porches de trois mètres de profondeur entre les chambres et les salles de bains. Quatre cyprès marquent le centre et les axes principaux du patio avant, et quatre autres sont alignés à l'intérieur du patio arrière. Un bassin creusé dans le sol souligne la limite de la maison « d'une extrémité à l'autre ».

A sketch by the architect seems to translate a greater complexity than that apparent in the forms and few openings of the house.

Eine Skizze des Architekten lässt auf größere Komplexität schließen, als die Formen und wenigen Öffnungen des Hauses vermuten lassen.

Un croquis de l'architecte témoigne d'une complexité plus grande que les formes et les rares ouvertures de la maison réalisée ne le laissent deviner.

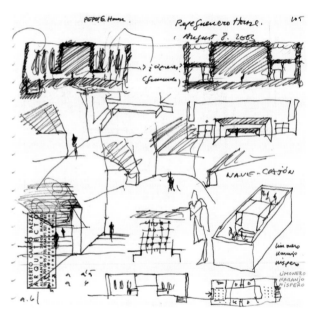

The exterior of the house is characterized by a radical simplicity that leaves the casual spectator wondering just what the function of this white block might be.

Das Äußere des Hauses zeichnet sich durch radikale Einfachheit aus, angesichts derer sich der zufällige Betrachter fragen mag, welche Funktion dieser weiße Block wohl haben könnte.

L'extérieur se caractérise par une simplicité radicale qui laisse le spectateur non averti se poser des questions sur la fonction de ce bloc immaculé.

The bright sun of Cádiz plays on the white forms, creating varying, geometric patterns, while the blue sky offers a striking contrast with the bleached purity of the architecture.

Die leuchtende Sonne von Cádiz malt Schatten auf die weißen Mauern und lässt dabei wechselnde geometrische Muster entstehen, während der tiefblaue Himmel einen starken Kontrast zur gebleichten Reinheit der Architektur bildet.

Le soleil éclatant de Cadix joue sur les formes architecturales pures et blanches et crée des motifs géométriques changeants sur le fond du ciel azur.

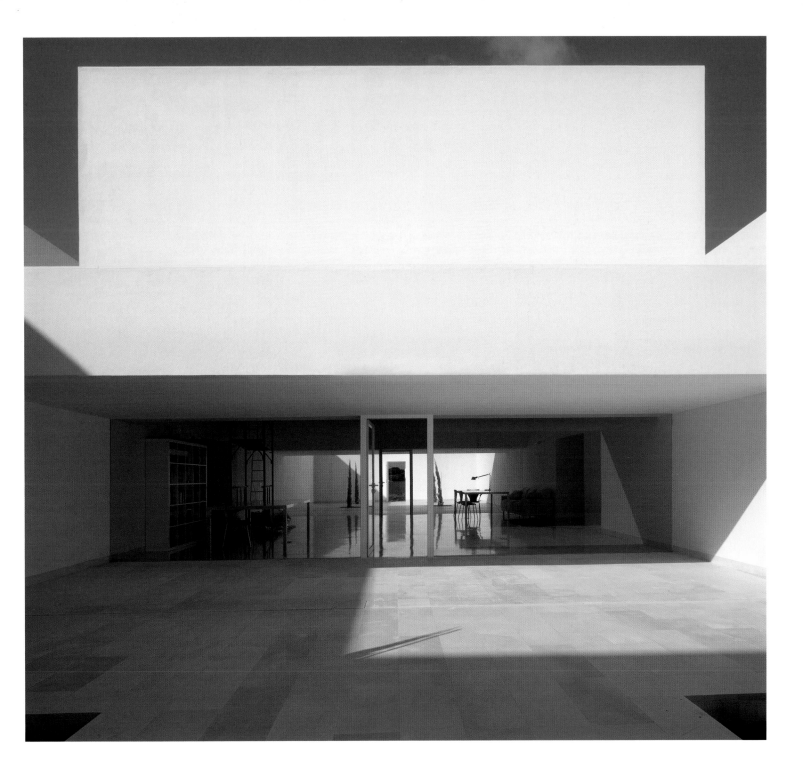

The overhanging blocks create shaded spaces in the sparsely furnished interior. Though the house is essentially open to the sky, it allows almost no view to the exterior at ground level.

Die vorspringenden Blöcke schaffen schattige Bereiche im spärlich möblierten Inneren. Obgleich das Haus im Grunde nach oben offen ist, gibt es im Erdgeschoss kaum Ausblicke auf den Außenraum.

Les blocs en porte-à-faux décrivent des espaces ombragés dans un intérieur meublé avec parcimonie. Essentiellement ouverte sur le ciel, la maison n'autorise pratiquement aucune perspective sur l'extérieur au niveau du sol.

Simple furniture and walls unencumbered by any form of decoration surely correspond to the architect's will to create a minimalist space. Single trees in the courtyard spaces confirm this reduction to essentials.

Schlichtes Mobiliar und von jeglichem Schmuck unbeeinträchtigte Wände entsprechen der Absicht des Architekten, einen minimalistischen Raum zu schaffen. Die einzelnen Bäume in den Innenhöfen unterstreichen diese Reduzierung auf das Essenzielle.

Les meubles simples et les murs non encombrés d'une quelconque décoration correspondent à la volonté de l'architecte de créer un espace minimaliste. Les quelques arbres de la cour confirment cette réduction à l'essentiel.

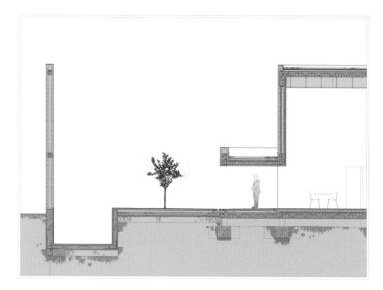
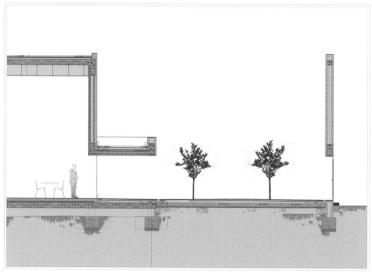

SANTIAGO CIRUGEDA

SANTIAGO CIRUGEDA
c/ Joaquín Costa, 7
41002 Seville

Tel: +34 670 79 44 09
Fax: +34 95 490 45 81
e-mail: sc@recetasurbanas.net
Web: www.recetasurbanas.net

SANTIAGO CIRUGEDA was born in Seville in 1971, and studied architecture at the Escuela Técnica Superior de Arquitectura in his native city. He calls himself a "citizen with the title of architect." His work has consisted in the production of a number of temporary, usually parasitic structures that call into question the very nature of architecture and its materials. He has participated extensively in debates, workshops, and exhibitions. He has frequently flirted with illegality in the realization of these projects, again questioning the rules that govern construction and urban development. He refers to a number of his projects as "strategies for subversive occupation." He participated in the 2003 Venice Biennale. His work includes: House Enlargement with Scaffolding, Seville (1998); Institutional Prothesis, Seville (1998–99); Puzzle House, the Closet Strategy, Seville (2002-03); and Trenches, Malaga Faculty of Fine Arts, Málaga (2005).

INSTITUTIONAL PROTHESIS, CENTER FOR CONTEMPORARY ARTS

CASTELLÓN 2004 - 05

CLIENT: Espai d'Art Contemporani de Castelló (EACC)
AREA: 143 m² for two classroom buildings, 181 m² sheets of floating concrete, 264 m² of left-over re-activated space
COST: €180 000
COLLABORATORS: Gianluca Stasi, Carlo Magoni
ACKNOWLEDGEMENTS: Lorenza Barboni, Juan de Nieves

Cirugeda proposed to create a new "wing" with classrooms for a museum, the Center for Contemporary Arts in Castellón, making use of an otherwise inaccessible terrace and filling a former concrete pond to make a public space in front of the museum. Intentionally calling on "improper" materials, he made use of black plastic formwork for pouring concrete floor slabs. As a critic has pointed out, to those who cannot identify these materials, they appear to have been intentionally designed for the extension. Load-bearing steel bars protrude from the formwork, holding the plastic elements, normally meant to be discarded, in place. There is both a criticism of "normal" architectural methods and production systems, and a willful discovery of the aesthetic qualities of utilitarian objects in this project. Intended for the production of "permanent" concrete floors, the formwork becomes the ephemeral expression of Cirugeda's interrogation of the nature of contemporary architecture. Cirugeda's "Recetas Urbanas" [urban prescriptions] propose the realization of such temporary and reversible "parasitic" projects, often even on the border of legality. Built in eight weeks, the addition has two main volumes measuring 60 and 80 m² respectively and two tunnels (30 m²). As a final gesture of questioning construction methods, Cirugeda has used the forms to create concrete slab benches.

Bei dem Anbau eines neuen Flügels mit Unterrichtsräumen für das Zentrum für Zeitgenössische Kunst in Castellón schlug Cirugeda vor, eine ansonsten unzugängliche Terrasse zu nutzen und ein Betonbecken aufzufüllen, um vor dem Museum einen öffentlichen Raum zu schaffen. Er entschied sich bewusst für „unpassende" Materialien und verwendete schwarze Schalungsformen aus Kunststoff, die dazu dienen, Bodenplatten aus Beton zu gießen. Ein Kritiker wies darauf hin, dass Nicht-Fachleute glauben könnten, diese Materialien seien eigens für den Anbau entwickelt worden. Stählerne Tragrippen ragen aus den Schalungsformen heraus und halten die Kunststoffelemente, die gewöhnlich entsorgt werden, an Ort und Stelle. Es geht bei diesem Projekt einerseits um die Kritik an „normalen" Bauverfahren und Produktionssystemen und andererseits um die gezielte Entdeckung der ästhetischen Qualitäten von Gebrauchsgütern. Die für die Produktion von „dauerhaften" Betonböden gedachten Schalungsformen werden zum vergänglichen Ausdruck von Cirugedas kritischer Einstellung zur zeitgenössischen Architektur. Cirugeda befürwortet in seinen „Recetas Urbanas" die Realisierung solch temporärer und reversibler „parasitischer" Projekte, die sich häufig am Rand der Legalität bewegen. Der in acht Wochen errichtete Anbau verfügt über zwei 60 und 80 m² große Bauteile sowie zwei Tunnelröhren (30 m²). Cirugeda stellt herkömmliche Bauverfahren endgültig in Frage, wenn er die Schalungsformen zur Herstellung von Sitzbänken aus Beton verwendet.

Cirugeda a proposé de créer cette nouvelle « aile » de salles de cours pour un musée, le Centre d'art contemporain de Castellón, en utilisant une terrasse par ailleurs inaccessible et en comblant un ancien bassin de béton pour dégager un espace public devant le musée. Faisant volontairement appel à des matériaux « impropres », il a utilisé des coffrages en plastique noir, servant au moulage de dalles de sol en béton. Comme l'a fait remarquer un critique pour ceux qui ne peuvent les identifier, ces éléments semblent avoir été intentionnellement fabriqués pour ce projet. Des tiges d'acier dépassent du coffrage pour maintenir en place ces éléments en plastique qui auraient normalement dû être jetés. On trouve ici à la fois une critique des méthodes « usuelles » de l'architecture et des systèmes de production « normaux » et une découverte volontariste des qualités esthétiques d'objets utilitaires. Conçu pour la fabrication de sols à vocation permanente, ce coffrage devient l'expression éphémère de l'interrogation de Cirugeda sur la nature de l'architecture contemporaine. Ses *Recetas urbanas* (recettes urbaines) proposent de réaliser des projets « parasites » temporaires et réversibles de ce type, souvent à la limite de la légalité. Construite en huit semaines, cette extension possède deux volumes principaux mesurant respectivement 60 et 80 m² et deux tunnels de 30 m². Dans son questionnement sur les méthodes de construction, l'architecte s'est aussi servi des coffrages pour créer des bancs en béton.

Cirugeda's interventions represent an implicit criticism of modern architecture but also an exploration of the potential uses of industrial materials.

Cirugedas Eingriffe beinhalten eine Kritik der modernen Architektur, aber auch die Erforschung möglicher Anwendungen von Industriematerialien.

Les interventions de Cirugeda expriment à la fois une critique implicite de l'architecture moderne et une exploration des usages potentiels des matériaux industriels.

By using unexpected materials or rather elements normally meant to be discarded, the architect questions the material reality of architecture and its expected appearance.

Indem er ungewöhnliche Materialien bzw. sonst zur Entsorgung vorgesehene Elemente verwendet, stellt der Architekt die materielle Realität von Architektur und ihr erwartetes Aussehen infrage.

En se servant de matériaux surprenants, ou surtout d'éléments normalement destinés à la déchetterie, l'architecte remet en question la réalité matérielle de l'architecture et ses aspects attendus.

ANTÓN GARCÍA-ABRIL

ANTÓN GARCÍA-ABRIL
& ENSAMBLE STUDIO
c/ Cristóbal Bordiú, 55, bajos
28003 Madrid

Tel: +34 91 541 08 48
e-mail: anton@ensamble.info
Web: www.ensamble.info

ANTÓN GARCÍA-ABRIL RUIZ was born in Madrid in 1969. He graduated from the ETSA in Madrid in Architecture and Urbanism in 1995 and went on to receive a doctorate from the same institution in 2000. He is currently a Professor of Architectural Projects at the ETSA. He worked in the office of Santiago Calatrava (1992) and in that of Alberto Campo Baeza (1990-94). He created his first firm in 1995, and his present one, Ensamble Studio, in 2000. García-Abril explains that the name of his firm is derived from a term used in architecture "assemble" and the musical term "ensemble." "This team," he says, "develops a multidisciplinary working scheme [...] to carry out the intervention of the architect in the whole process that leads to the artistic work, from the conceptual abstraction to the construction detail." Essentially this means that he has created an in-house contracting firm. His completed projects include the Musical Studies Center (Santiago de Compostela, 2002); Concert Hall and Music School (Medina del Campo, 2003); Martemar House (Málaga, 2003-05); Valdés Studio (Madrid, 2004), all in Spain. Amongst his current projects: SGAE Central Office (Santiago de Compostela, 2005); Berklee Tower of Music (Valencia, 2007); La Casa del Lector Library (Madrid, 2006); Hemeroscopium House (Madrid, 2006); Liric Theater (Mexico D.F., 2007); Fleta Theater (Zaragoza, 2007); Paraíso Theater (Shanghai, China, 2007).

MUSICAL STUDIES CENTER
SANTIAGO DE COMPOSTELA
2002

CLIENT: Consortium of the City of Santiago
AREA: 1700 m²
TECHNICAL ARCHITECT: Javier Cuesta
COLLABORATORS: Bernardo Angelini, Eduardo
Martin Asunción, Arantxa Osés, Débora Mesa,
Andrés Toledo, Guillermo Sevillano

This unusual building is located in the Vista Alegre green area near the historic center of Santiago de Compostela where there are a number of academic and research facilities. Intended for postgraduate studies and the training of members of the Galician Orchestra, its forms were suggested not only by this function but also by the proximity of a pavilion designed by César Portela "made of the same materials and of similar dimensions." As the architect points out, from a distance, the building looks more like a monolithic block of rough granite than anything else. From the middle ground, he says that the structure's "rhythm of seven parts" becomes visible. "We move closer and the shape is broken," he says, "the pieces jump, expressing its abrasive materiality and defining holes which define the constructive scales of the building, incisions of light that tear the façade [and] transform a hole into a shadow which speaks of the subtraction of mass by light in a vertical element, while the two big perforations are a direct result of the large interior volume." The interior articulation of the building was determined on the whole by the acoustic requirements of the practice rooms. It may be the roughness of the granite that gives something of an ancient feeling to this structure. The architect says, "There's a search for the constructive expression of stone that we have learned from history, going back to Egypt and Rome... It seems that the building was always there."

Dieses ungewöhnliche Gebäude liegt im Grünzug Vista Alegre in der Nähe des historischen Zentrums von Santiago de Compostela, wo eine Reihe von Akademien und Forschungseinrichtungen ihren Sitz haben. Es ist gedacht für weiterführende Studiengänge und als Probengebäude für Mitglieder des galicischen Orchesters. Seine Gestaltung ergab sich nicht nur durch diese Funktionen, sondern auch durch die Nähe zu einem von César Portela „mit den gleichen Materialien und in ähnlichen Dimensionen" erbauten Pavillon. Der Architekt weist darauf hin, dass der Bau aus der Ferne am ehesten wie ein monolithischer Block unbehauenen Granits aussieht. Aus mittlerer Entfernung, sagt er, erkenne man „den siebenbenteiligen Rhythmus" des Bauwerks. „Wir nähern uns und die Form zerbricht, die Teile springen und bringen so ihre schroffe Materialität zum Ausdruck; sie definieren Öffnungen, die den konstruktiven Maßstab des Gebäudes bestimmen, Einschnitte von Licht, die die Fassade zerreißen... [und] eine Öffnung in einen Schatten verwandeln, der von der Subtraktion von Masse durch Licht in einem vertikalen Element zeugt, während die beiden großen Perforationen die direkte Folge des ausgedehnten Innenraums sind." Die Gliederung des Inneren wurde im Großen und Ganzen durch die akustischen Anforderungen der Probenräume bestimmt. Vielleicht ist es die Rauheit des Granits, der das Gebäude seine nahezu antike Anmutung verdankt. Dazu meint der Architekt: „Es gibt eine Suche nach dem tektonischen Ausdruck von Stein, die wir aus der Geschichte bis zurück zu den Ägyptern und Römern gelernt haben ... Es scheint, als habe der Bau schon immer dort gestanden."

Cet étonnant bâtiment destiné aux études musicales supérieures et aux répétitions des membres de l'Orchestre de Galice est situé dans la zone verte de Vista Alegre, proche du centre historique de Saint-Jacques-de-Compostelle où se trouvent déjà un certain nombre de bâtiments universitaires et de recherche. Ses formes ont été suggérées non seulement par sa fonction mais aussi par la proximité d'un pavillon conçu par César Portela « dans les mêmes matériaux et de dimensions similaires ». L'architecte fait remarquer que de loin, le bâtiment fait d'abord penser à un monolithe de granit brut. « En s'approchant, dit-il, le rythme [de la structure], en sept parties, devient lisible. La forme éclate, les parties qui la composent surgissent, expriment sa matérialité abrasive, et déterminent des trous qui définissent les échelles, des incisions de lumière qui déchirent la façade... [et] transforment un trou en ombre qui nous parle de soustraction de la masse par la lumière dans un élément vertical, tandis que deux grandes perforations résultent directement du dessin du vaste volume intérieur. » En général, l'articulation intérieure a été déterminée par les contraintes acoustiques des salles de musique. Le caractère brut du granit crée éventuellement une impression d'ancienneté, que confirme l'architecte : « On trouve ici une recherche de l'expression constructive de la pierre que nous avons apprise de l'Histoire, en remontant jusqu'à l'Egypte et Rome... Il semble que le bâtiment ait toujours été là. »

The extremely regular square plan of the structure is visible in the drawings to the left, with part of the building below grade (sections below). The rough exterior surface gives an almost medieval feeling to the building.

Der äußerst regelmäßige quadratische Grundriss des Bauwerks ist auf den Zeichnungen links zu sehen, auf den Schnitten unten der unter Planum liegende Teil. Die roh zugerichteten Außenmauern verleihen dem Gebäude eine fast mittelalterliche Anmutung.

Plan en forme de carré régulier, à gauche, et coupe montrant la partie du bâtiment en sous-sol (ci-dessous). La surface laissée brute donne une impression de construction quasi-médiévale.

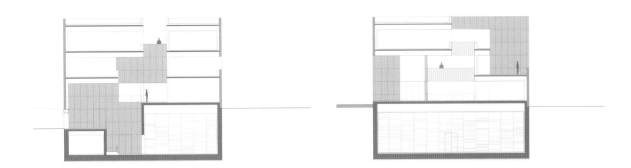

The rough stone exterior is contrasted with these modern interior spaces, with natural light entering from the upper skylights.

Die roh belassenen Steinmauern stehen in Kontrast zu diesen modernen Innenräumen, in die durch Oberlichter Helligkeit einfällt.

L'extérieur en pierre brute contraste avec les volumes intérieurs très modernes. La lumière naturelle pénètre par des verrières zénithales.

MANUEL VALDÉS STUDIO
MADRID
2004

CLIENT: Manuel Valdés Blasco
AREA: 900 m²
TECHNICAL ARCHITECT: Javier Cuesta
COLLABORATORS: Ignacio Marí,
Johannes Gramse

Built with galvanized steel profiles, a galvanized steel roof, grey concrete floors and interior cladding made of Lexan 76-18 polycarbonate, the Manuel Valdés Studio is exceedingly simple, and as the architect readily admits, it is something of a cosmetic project. Working with an industrial warehouse, Anton García-Abril determined that the best solution was to veil the unwanted complexities of the architecture. As he writes, "Sometimes architecture is all about covering up. A space can be well proportioned yet full of elements which alter the ambience and fill it with noise. This can be transformed by using a simple trick: dressing up the space. The key is an elegant covering that can define a space's proportions, create a special light and draw attention to specific details. It will promote the attractive features and hide the undesirable ones behind a light pleated plastic veil. This straightforward operation converts an ugly and plain industrial warehouse into a suggestive architectural area where sculptures can be exhibited. It is a well lit, clean and neutral space that makes difficult sculpting work easier. The translucid polycarbonate Lexan covering allows us to unite all the areas of the warehouse. The external spaces become work and exhibition areas while the warehouse as a whole improves."

Das mit verzinkten Stahlprofilen, einem verzinkten Stahldach, grauen Betonböden und einer Innenverkleidung aus Lexan 76-18 Polycarbonat ausgestattete Atelier von Manuel Valdés mutet außerordentlich schlicht an und der Architekt gesteht freimütig, dass es sich gewissermaßen um ein kosmetisches Projekt handelt. Da er es mit einem Industrielagerhaus zu tun hatte, entschied García-Abril, die beste Lösung sei es, die unerwünschten Problemstellen der Architektur zu verschleiern. Dazu führt er aus: „Bisweilen geht es bei der Architektur vor allem ums Verbergen. Ein gut proportionierter Raum kann voller Elemente sein, die das Ambiente verändern und mit Lärm erfüllen. Dies kann man durch einen einfachen Trick ändern: indem man den Raum herausputzt. Entscheidend ist eine elegante Verkleidung, die die Proportionen eines Raums bestimmen, ein besonderes Licht schaffen und die Aufmerksamkeit auf bestimmte Details lenken kann. Sie

wird die reizvollen Merkmale hervorheben und die unerwünschten mit einem leichten, gefalteten Kunststoffschleier kaschieren. Dieses unkomplizierte Verfahren verwandelt ein hässliches, unansehnliches Industrielagerhaus in einen anregenden architektonischen Raum, in dem man Skulpturen ausstellen kann. Es ist ein gut ausgeleuchteter, sauberer, neutraler Raum, der die schwierige Bildhauerei einfacher macht. Die lichtdurchlässige Polycarbonathülle aus Lexan macht es möglich, sämtlichen Innenräumen des Lagerhauses ein einheitliches Gepräge zu verleihen. Die Außenräume werden zu Arbeits- und Ausstellungsbereichen, während das Lagerhaus als Ganzes gewinnt."

Excessivement simple, le studio de Manuel Valdés qui fait appel à des profilés, une toiture en acier galvanisé, des sols en béton gris et un habillage intérieur en polycarbonate Lexan 76-18 constitue presque un projet cosmétique, ce que l'architecte est prêt à reconnaître. Travaillant sur la base d'un entrepôt industriel existant, Anton García-Abril a pensé que la meilleure solution était de masquer les complexités inutiles de sa construction : « Parfois l'architecture consiste aussi à masquer les choses. Un espace peut être bien proportionné, mais bourré d'éléments qui altèrent l'atmosphère et font du « bruit ». On peut alors modifier cette situation par un procédé tout simple : habiller l'espace. La clé consiste à trouver un habillage élégant qui contribue à la définition des proportions du volume, crée un éclairage particulier et attire l'attention sur quelques détails spécifiques. Ainsi fait-on ressortir les caractéristiques les plus séduisantes et dissimule-t-on celles dont on ne veut pas derrière un voile de plastique plissé. Cette opération simple transforme un entrepôt industriel laid et banal en un espace architectural dans lequel il est possible d'exposer des sculptures. C'est un espace bien éclairé, net et neutre, qui facilite le travail difficile du sculpteur. La couverture en polycarbonate translucide Lexan nous a permis d'unifier les différentes parties de l'entrepôt. Les espaces externes deviennent des aires de travail et d'exposition tandis que l'entrepôt en tant que tel est amélioré. »

A drawing and an image highlight the extreme, indeed minimalist, simplicity of the design, based on an industrial warehouse, but transformed in part by the extensive use of corrugated polycarbonate sheets.

Zeichnung und Abbildung vermitteln die minimalistische Einfachheit dieses Entwurfs, der auf einem Industrielagerhaus basiert, das durch den umfassenden Gebrauch von Platten aus gewelltem Polycarbonat verwandelt wurde.

Un plan et une vue mettent en valeur la simplicité extrême, voire minimaliste, du projet réalisé à partir d'un entrepôt industriel existant, mais transformé par l'utilisation de panneaux de polycarbonate ondulé.

The vertical alignment of the polycarbonate sheets gives a structured rigor to the simple forms of the building, where no extra detailing has been allowed.

Die vertikale Ausrichtung der Polycarbonat-platten strukturiert die einfachen Formen des Gebäudes und erlaubt keine weitere Detaillierung.

L'alignement vertical des plaques de poly-carbonate insuffle une structuration rigou-reuse dans les formes simples du bâtiment. Aucun détail superflu n'a été autorisé.

Vertical slats allow natural light into the space through the walls, while horizontal openings on the roof serve the same function. The basic space is extremely simple, the architectural innovation is in the materials and the lighting.

Durch vertikale Schlitze in den Mauern und horizontale Öffnungen im Dach fällt Tageslicht in das Gebäude ein. Das grundlegende Quadrat ist sehr einfach, die architektonische Innovation betrifft Materialien und Beleuchtung.

Des ouvertures verticales dans les murs et horizontales en toiture laissent pénétrer la lumière naturelle. Le volume est d'une simplicité extrême. L'innovation architecturale réside dans les matériaux et l'éclairage.

7

RAFAEL DE LA-HOZ

RAFAEL DE LA-HOZ
ARQUITECTOS
Paseo de la Castellana, 82, 2º A
28046 Madrid

Tel: +34 91 74 53 50 0
Fax: +34 91 56 17 80 3
e-mail: estudio@rafaeldelahoz.com
Web: www.rafaeldelahoz.com

Born in Córdoba in 1955, **RAFAEL DE LA-HOZ CASTANYS** obtained his Diploma in Architecture from the Escuela Técnica Superior de Arquitectura in Madid and went on to get a Master's degree from the Polytechnic University of Madrid (1981). He is the director of the studio Rafael de La-Hoz Architects. His main recent and built work includes: the "Parque Norte" Business Park, Madrid (2000-01); "Encina Real", 60 housing units in the "Encinar de los Reyes", Madrid (2001-02); the Office Headquarters of Vodafone Madrid (2001-02); the "Bilma" Business Park, Madrid (2001-03); Pentax Offices (2001-03); the Main Offices of Endesa in Madrid (1999-2003); the Municipal Meeting Facilities of the District of Retiro, Madrid (2002-04); the Higher Council of Chambers of Commerce Headquarters, Madrid (2002-04); Master Plan Vilamoura, Algarve, Portugal (2004); the Main Offices of the Madrid legal firm Uría Menéndez (2003-05); a sustainable called "Pórtico", currently the headquarters of Marsans, Madrid (2003-05); BMW Madrid (2004-05); the Auditorium of the Spanish Olympic Committee, Madrid (2004-05); an Office Building for Bouygues Development, Madrid (2005); Offices of the Madrid legal firm Garrigues (2003-06). His current work includes: District C of Telefónica, Las Tablas, Madrid (2004-2007); Repsol Headquarters (2007-09); Emilio Vargas Hotel, Madrid (2005-07); "Rafael del Pino" Foundation Offices, Madrid (2005-07); Children's Theatre and Arts Centre "Daoiz y Velarde", Madrid (2007-09); the Hércules Towers in "Los Barrios", Cádiz (2006-08); CECO Main Offices and Training Facilities, Córdoba (2006-08); the Tower of Freedom in Gdansk, Poland (2007-10); the Extension plan for the Vilamoura Marina, Algarve, Portugal (2007-09); Gran Vía Building, Madrid (2006-08); Chamartín Towers, Madrid (2007-10); and Juvenil Court—Campus of Justice—in Madrid (2007-10).

HIGHER COUNCIL OF CHAMBERS OF COMMERCE

MADRID 2002 - 04

CLIENT: Higher Council of
Chambers of Commerce
AREA: 5800 m² below ground +
2900 m² above ground
COST: €9 000 000
COLLABORATORS: Silvia Villamor, Ángel Rolán,
Manuel Doménech, Elena Elósegui

Rafael de La-Hoz begins his description of this structure with a bit of linguistics or semantics. "Architecture builds ideas, but also, occasionally, meanings," he says. "Paradoxically, the idea behind this project is precisely to build only meanings. In German, the word *Kammer* designates a place to meet or assemble, whereas the word *Kamera* is used to refer to a photographic camera. Similarly, in English, *Chamber of Commerce* refers to the place where businessmen meet and the word *camera* refers to a device for recording a visual image. All these words derive from the same root, which is related to the words 'box' or 'chamber', although there are subtle differences. In Spanish, however, the same word *cámara* is used for both a place of assembly and a photographic device. So in this case, the Spanish word is more ambiguous [...] The theme of this project is precisely this ambiguous meaning. It can be said that the construction is built to both accommodate and capture." The architect goes on to suggest that he has set aside "the conceptual interpretations and suppositions" that have to do with the site and the logic of construction to concentrate on making the two simultaneous meanings of the word *cámara* compatible. He sets a pure, geometric solid form on a horizontal plane. Three openings allow light to enter the chamber and visitors to see specific, framed views "as though they were the shutters of a camera." A total of three spaces are thus created, "representing the meanings of both meeting and seeing."

Rafael de La-Hoz beginnt seine Beschreibung dieses Gebäudes mit ein wenig Linguistik oder Semantik. „Architektur baut Ideen, aber bisweilen auch Bedeutungen", sagt er. „Paradoxerweise geht es bei der Idee hinter diesem Projekt genau darum, Bedeutungen zu bauen. Im Deutschen bezeichnet das Wort ‚Kammer' einen Ort, an dem man sich treffen oder versammeln kann. Dagegen ist ‚Kamera' gleichbedeutend mit Fotoapparat. Ähnlich verhält es sich im Englischen, wo ‚Chamber of Commerce' den Ort bezeichnet, an dem sich Geschäftsleute treffen und ‚camera' ein Gerät zum Aufzeichnen von Bildern. Diesen Worten liegt derselbe Wortstamm zugrunde. Im Spanischen bezeichnet das gleiche Wort ‚cámara' allerdings sowohl einen Versammlungsraum als auch einen Fotoapparat. In diesem Fall ist das spanische Wort also zweideutig [...] Thema dieses Projekts ist genau diese Zweideutigkeit. Man könnte sagen, dass der Bau gleichermaßen entstand, um unterzubringen und einzufangen." Der Architekt gibt des Weiteren zu verstehen, dass er die mit dem Standort und der konstruktiven Logik zusammenhängenden „konzeptuellen Interpretationen und Voraussetzungen" ausgeklammert hat, um sich darauf zu konzentrieren, die unterschiedlichen Bedeutungen des Wortes „cámara" kompatibel zu machen. Er stellt einen rein geometrischen Körper auf eine horizontale Fläche. Durch drei Öffnungen fällt Licht in die „Kammer" und lässt Besucher bestimmte, gerahmte Ansichten sehen, „als ob sie Blenden an einer Kamera wären". Dadurch entstehen drei Räume, „die die Bedeutung von Treffen und Sehen verkörpern".

Rafael de La-Hoz entame la description de ce projet par quelques considérations linguistiques ou sémantiques : « L'architecture construit des idées, mais aussi, à l'occasion, du sens. Paradoxalement, l'idée à la base de ce projet est précisément de ne construire que du sens. En allemand, le mot de *Kammer* désigne un lieu où se rencontrer, ou se réunir, alors que celui de *kamera* désigne un appareil photo. De même, en anglais, *Chamber of Commerce* se réfère à un lieu où les hommes d'affaires se rencontrent, et la *camera* est un appareil qui permet d'enregistrer une image. Tous ces mots proviennent de la même racine, liée aux mots « boîte » ou « chambre », bien que l'on trouve entre eux quelques différences subtiles. En Espagne, cependant, le même mot, *cámara*, est utilisé à la fois pour un lieu de réunions et un appareil photographique. Ainsi, le mot espagnol est-il plus ambigu [...] Le thème de ce projet est précisément cette ambiguïté de signification. On peut dire que le projet a été réalisé à la fois pour recevoir et pour capter. » L'architecte suggère ensuite qu'il a écarté « les interprétations et suppositions conceptuelles » en relation avec le site et la logique de construction pour se concentrer sur la mise en œuvre des deux significations compatibles du mot *cámara*. Il a établi une forme pure, géométrique et fermée sur un plan horizontal. Trois ouvertures permettent à la lumière d'y pénétrer et aux visiteurs de percevoir des vues spécifiques et cadrées « comme par les volets d'une caméra ». Trois volumes sont ainsi créés « proposant le sens à la fois de réunir et de voir ».

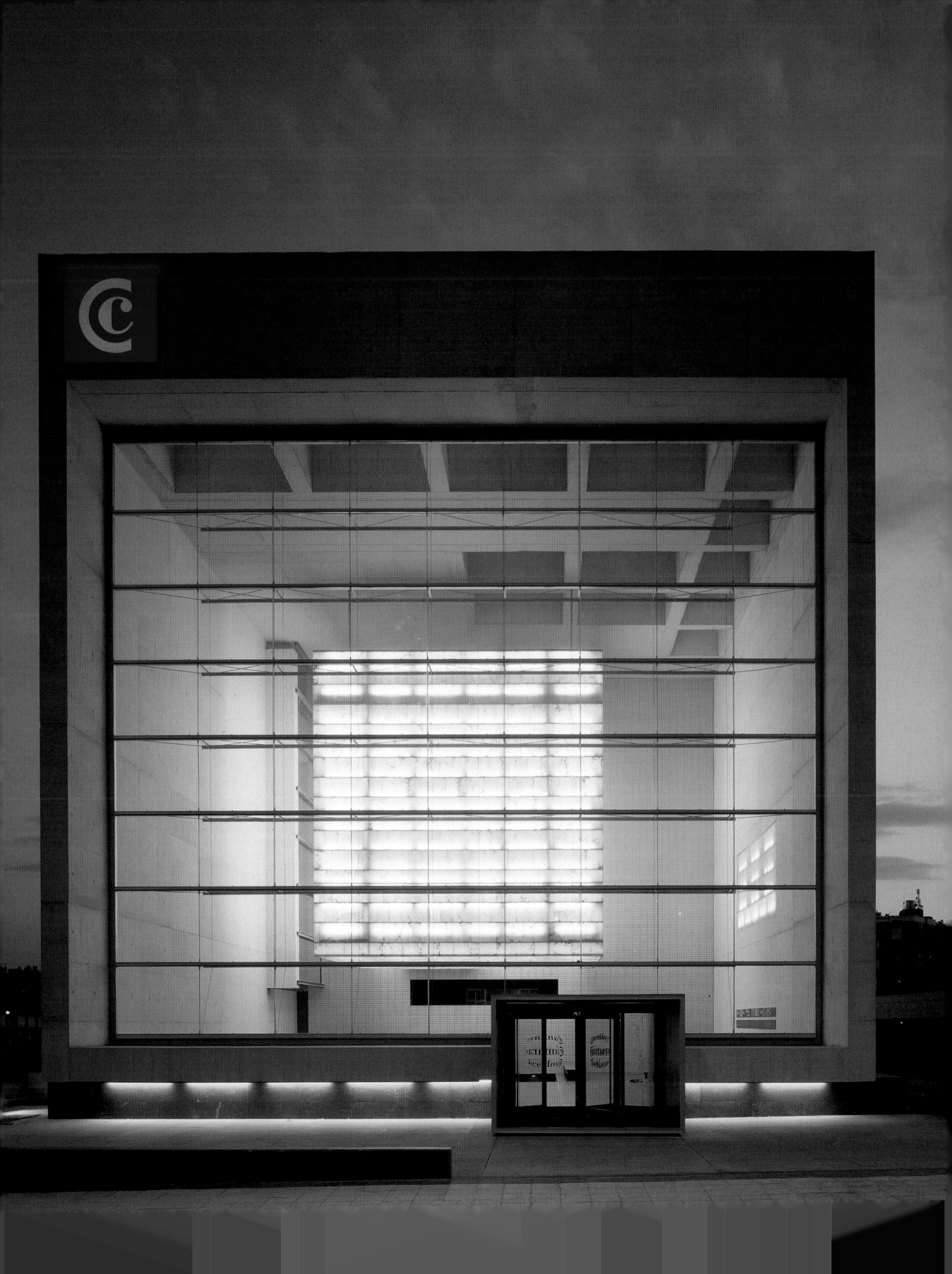

The solidity of the building surely reflects its function, linked to the businesses of Madrid, and the architect links its box-like form to the origins of the word "chamber" as in Chamber of Commerce.

Das massiv wirkende Gebäude reflektiert seine mit dem Madrider Geschäftsleben assoziierte Funktion, und der Architekt verbindet die Kastenform mit den Ursprüngen des Wortes „Kammer" wie bei Handelskammer.

La massivité du bâtiment reflète sa fonction liée au monde des affaires de Madrid. L'architecte a pris au mot le « chambre » de Chambre de commerce.

The interior architecture is characterized by a willful contrast between opaque and transparent surfaces, or a play on weight and lightness (right).

Die Innenarchitektur kennzeichnet der bewusste Kontrast zwischen opaken und transparenten Oberflächen oder das Spiel mit Schwere und Leichtigkeit (rechts).

L'architecture intérieure se caractérise par un contraste recherché entre les surfaces opaques et transparentes, ainsi que par un jeu entre gravité et légèreté (à droite).

8

JOSEP LLINAS

JOSEP LLINAS
Avinguda República Argentina, 74, entl.
08023 Barcelona

Tel: +34 93 213 10 98
Fax: +34 93 285 53 69
e-mail: llinas@coac.net

JOSEP LLINÀS was born in Castellón de la Plana in 1945. He graduated with a degree in architecture from the Escuela Técnica Superior de Arquitectura in Barcelona (ETSAB) in 1969. He has taught in various institutions including the École Poly-technique Fédérale of Lausanne as well as the ETSAs of Barcelona and Pamplona. His built work includes the Cerdanyola-Ripollet Health Center, Barcelona (1982-85); School and Library of Engineering, Barcelona (1987-89); Tomas Y. Valiente Lecture Building, Barcelona (1993-96); Town Planning, Plaça de Sant Augustí Vell, Barcelona (1998/2002-05); Vila de Gracia Library, Barcelona (2000-02); Can Ginesta Library, Barcelona (2001-03); Fort Pienc Block, Barcelona (2001-03); and Buildings B and C, Facility 7, Can Jaumandreu Block, Barcelona (2003-05). Recent projects include: a Winery in Mendivil, Pamplona (2002-); Barcelona Institute of Ocular Microsurgery, Barcelona (2004-); and single-family houses in Vila-Seca, Barcelona (2005-) and Llinars del Vallès, Barcelona (2005-); and extensions to the Viladecans Town Hall, Barcelona (1998/2005-).

JAUME FUSTER LIBRARY
BARCELONA 2001 - 05

CLIENT: Barcelona Town Hall, District of Gracia
AREA: 5026 m²
COST: €2 680 513 (first phase); €5 826 347 (second phase)
COLLABORATOR: Joan Vera Garcia
ASSISTANTS: Roger Subira i Ezquerra, Carlos Cachon
Martinez and Andrea Tissino

The architect explains that the unusual shape of this building is the result of an effort to "merge the library volume with the buildings around it." The part of the building that opens onto Plaza Lesseps is lower and appears to shelter and invite visitors. The wood cladding of the lower faces of the overhanging entrance canopies accentuate a feeling of warmth implied by the sweeping, angled forms. Stone, gray metal, and wood alternate in this inventive and dynamic design that does indeed appear to have a direct relationship to its site. The rising volumes of the library in a sense symbolize the movement of the city from the Collserola mountains to the square which is "the end or starting point"—a "mountain-city boundary." Given the importance of the mountains to the city, this relationship is a fundamental one, linking the setting to the architecture in a fundamental way. The rhomboid floor plan of the building translates its vertical movements into the horizontal plane. Despite the obliquely angled exterior walls, the interior design is both logical and simple, with a good deal of natural light and frequent views from one level toward another.

Der Architekt erklärt die ungewöhnliche Form dieses Gebäudes als Ergebnis des Versuchs, „den Bibliotheksbau mit der gebauten Umgebung zu verschmelzen". Der Teil des Gebäudes, der sich zur Plaza Lesseps hin öffnet, ist niedriger und scheint die Besucher zugleich zu schützen und hereinzubitten. Die unteren Stirnseiten der freitragenden Vordächer über dem Eingang sind mit Holz verschalt. Dies unterstreicht das durch die ausgreifenden, winkligen Formen hervorgerufene Gefühl der Geborgenheit. Bei diesem innovativen, dynamischen Entwurf, der tatsächlich einen direkten Bezug zu seinem Standort zu haben scheint, wechseln sich Stein, graues Metall und Holz ab. Die aufsteigenden Baukörper der Bibliothek ver-

körpern in gewissem Sinn die Bewegung der Stadt von den Collserola-Bergen zu dem Platz, der „das Ende oder den Ausgangspunkt" markiert – „Schnittstelle zwischen Bergen und Stadt". Angesichts der Bedeutung der Berge für die Stadt, ist diese Beziehung eine grundlegende, die die Architektur auf fundamentale Weise mit der Szenerie verknüpft. Der rhombenförmige Grundriss des Gebäudes überträgt seine Vertikalbewegungen auf die horizontale Fläche. Trotz der schrägwinkligen Außenwände zeichnet sich die Gestaltung des Inneren durch Logik und Schlichtheit, reichlich Tageslicht und häufige Blickachsen von einer Ebene zur anderen aus.

Pour l'architecte, cette forme étonnante est l'aboutissement d'une recherche de « fusion du volume de la bibliothèque avec les immeubles qui l'entourent ». La partie surbaissée du bâtiment qui donne sur la place Lesseps invite et protège à la fois les visiteurs. L'habillage de bois des sous-faces des auvents de l'entrée accentue le sentiment de chaleur de l'accueil que suggèrent déjà les formes arrondies et inclinées. La pierre, le métal gris et le bois alternent dans ce projet inventif et dynamique qui semble entretenir une relation directe avec son site. En un sens, l'élévation des volumes de cette bibliothèque symbolise le mouvement qui anime la topographie barcelonaise entre la place Lesseps qui est « une fin ou un point de départ », « une frontière ville-montagne », et les montagnes de Collserola. Quand on sait l'importance de l'environnement montagneux à Barcelone, la relation créée entre l'architecture et son cadre est ici fondamentale. Le plan au sol en losange traduit horizontalement ce mouvement. Malgré la découpe en oblique de certains murs extérieurs, l'aménagement intérieur est à la fois logique et simple, l'éclairage naturel abondant et les perspectives entre les niveaux fréquentes.

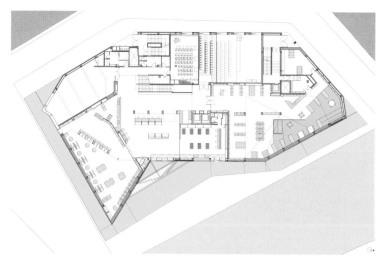 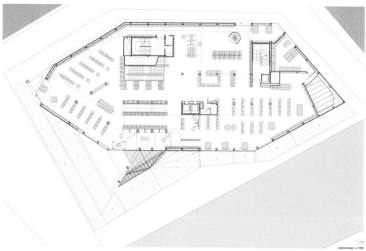

The plan of the library adapts to its irregular site (above and below). The building helps to create the public square near its entrance and uses its front canopy to invite passersby to enter.

Der Grundriss der Bibliothek passt sich dem unregelmäßigen Baugrund an (oben und unten). Das Gebäude ist an der Entstehung des öffentlichen Platzes unweit seines Eingangs beteiligt und nutzt sein Vordach, um Passanten hereinzulocken.

Le plan de la bibliothèque s'est adapté à son terrain irrégulier (ci-dessus et ci-dessous). Le bâtiment génère par sa forme une petite place devant l'entrée. L'auvent au-dessus de celle-ci est une invitation adressée aux passants.

Echoing the nearby hills, the building rises in the direction of the city's topography. Stone and glass dominate the cladding of the structure, making it fit in with the stone plaza.

Die nahe gelegenen Hügel aufgreifend, vollzieht der aufsteigende Bau die topografische Bewegung der Stadt nach. Das überwiegend mit Stein und Glas verkleidete Gebäude passt gut zum mit Platten belegten Platz.

En rappel aux collines avoisinantes, le bâtiment s'élève dans l'orientation générale de la topographie. La pierre et le verre qui constituent l'essentiel de l'habillage extérieur viennent en harmonie avec le dallage de pierre de la place.

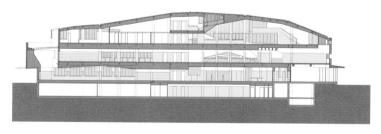

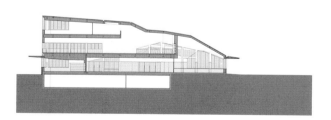

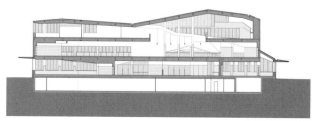

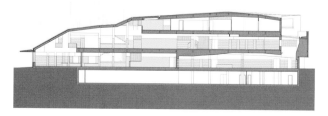

FRANCISCO MANGADO

FRANCISCO MANGADO
Vuelta del Castillo, 5, ático
31007 Pamplona (Navarra)

Tel: +34 948 27 62 02
Fax: +34 948 17 65 0 5
e-mail: mangado@fmangado.com
Web: www.fmangado.com

FRANCISCO MANGADO was born in Estella, Navarra, in 1957 and obtained his architectural degree in 1981 from the Escuela de Arquitectura de la Universidad de Navarra. From the beginning of his career, Mangado combined academic duties with the professional activity at his Pamplona studio. He has taught at the University of Navarra, University of Texas (Arlington), Harvard Graduate School of Design, and at the International University of Catalunya. His most significant projects include: the Mikaela House, Gorraiz, Navarra (1997); Pools in La Coruña (1998); Plaza de Dalí, Madrid (1999); offices for the University of Navarra (2000); Guipúzcoa Center for Technical Studies and Research, San Sebastián (2001); Baluarte Auditorium and Convention Center, Pamplona, Navarra (published here; 2000–03); Archaeological Museum of Vitoria (2002–); Ávila Exhibition and Convention Center (2002–); Manduca Restaurant, Madrid (2003); Teulada Municipal Auditorium, Alicante (2004); offices for Gamesa Eólica (2003–); Center for the Development of New Technologies in Galicia, Santiago de Compostela (2004–); Football Stadium in Palencia (2005–); Palma Convention Center and Hotel (2005); and the Spanish Pavilion for the International Expo in Zaragoza (2008).

BALUARTE CONVENTION CENTER AND AUDITORIUM OF NAVARRA

PAMPLONA 2000 - 03

CLIENT: Government of Navarra
AREA: 65 000 m²
COST: €75 000 000
ASSOCIATED ARCHITECT: Alfonso Alzugaray Los Arcos
COLLABORATORS: Carlos Pereda, Isabel López,
María Langarita, Laura Martínez de Gereñu

Described as the most important architectural project undertaken in the "recent history of Navarra," the Baluarte Center is located over an old fortress and occupies a site at the point of transition from the historic center of Pamplona and its periphery. The architect has insisted on the "urban calling" of the complex, with a large square that in some sense enters the building itself. The L-shaped layout contains a larger auditorium seating 1744 people in its west wing. A smaller auditorium is "tucked into the angle formed by the intersection of the two wings." The main access and foyer are situated between the two largely autonomous wings. Exhibition spaces are located on the Avenida del Ejército side at ground level and below grade. Some remnants of the old fortress, the Baluarte de San Antón are displayed in the underground areas. Three halls for small conferences or concerts are located below the main auditorium. Façades are clad in black quartzite, gray granite paving slabs are used in the square, while warmer materials such as beech or the rare Ipe wood are used inside.

Das als wichtigstes Architekturprojekt „in der jüngeren Geschichte Navarras" bezeichnete Kongresszentrum Baluarte befindet sich über einer alten Festung und damit auf einem Gelände am Übergang vom historischen Zentrum Pamplonas zur Peripherie. Der Architekt beharrt mit einem großflächigen Platz, der gewissermaßen selbst das Gebäude betritt, auf der „urbanen Berufung" des Komplexes. Im Westflügel des L-förmigen Gebäudes ist ein großes Auditorium mit 1744 Plätzen untergebracht. Ein kleinerer Saal „liegt im Schnittpunkt der beiden Flügel". Der Hauptzugang und das Foyer befinden sich zwischen den beiden weitgehend autonomen Bauteilen. An der Seite zur Avenida del Ejército liegen Ausstellungsräume im Erdgeschoss sowie unter Planum. In den unterirdischen Bereichen sind Reste der alten Festung Baluarte de San Antón zu sehen. Drei Hallen für kleinere Konferenzen oder Konzerte befinden sich unter dem Hauptauditorium. Die Fassaden sind mit schwarzem Quarzit verkleidet, der Platz ist mit grauem Granit gepflastert, während im Inneren wärmere Materialien wie Buchenholz oder das brasilianische Ipêholz verwendet wurden.

Présenté comme le plus important projet architectural de « l'histoire récente de la Navarre », ce palais des congrès est situé dans l'emprise d'une ancienne forteresse, à un point de transition entre le centre historique de Pampelune et sa périphérie. L'architecte insiste sur « la vocation urbaine » de ce complexe donnant sur une vaste place qui, d'une certaine façon pénètre dans le bâtiment. Le plan en « L » regroupe un grand auditorium de 1744 places dans l'aile droite et un plus petit « niché dans l'angle à l'intersection des deux ailes ». L'accès principal et le hall d'entrée sont situés entre les deux ailes en grande partie autonomes. Les salles d'exposition au rez-de-chaussée et en sous-sol donnent sur l'Avenida de Ejército. Certains vestiges de la vieille forteresse ont été conservés dans les zones souterraines. Trois petites salles destinées à accueillir des conférences ou des concerts se trouvent sous l'auditorium principal. Les façades sont habillées de quartzite noir, la place de pavés de granit et des matériaux plus chaleureux, comme le bouleau ou le bois d'ipé, sont utilisés à l'intérieur.

PALACIO DE CONGRESOS Y AUDITORIO DE NAVARRA

Images of the Convention Center and an architect's sketch (below) give an impression of solid, rigorously carved blocks of stone that hover in the air.

Bilder des Kongresszentrums und eine Skizze des Architekten (unten) vermitteln den Eindruck massiver, exakt beschnittener Steinblöcke, die scheinbar über dem Boden schweben.

Les vues du palais des congrès et un croquis de l'architecte (ci-dessous) donnent l'impression de blocs de pierre sculptés suspendus dans les airs.

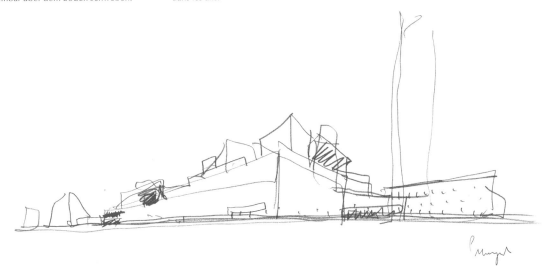

Section drawings show the largely rectilinear design in another light, revealing the hollow blocks that appear so solid from the outside. The exterior (above) is rigorous and apparently quite closed with open strips at the bottom and top.

Schnittzeichnungen zeigen den größtenteils geradlinigen Entwurf in anderem Licht, indem die von außen so massiv wirkenden Hohlkörper sichtbar werden. Der oben zu sehende Außenbau wirkt streng und recht geschlossen, mit oben und unten je einem offenen Streifen.

Les coupes montrent l'orthogonalité rigoureuse des plans sous un autre éclairage ; elles montrent aussi que les blocs, qui semblent massifs vus de l'extérieur, sont creux. L'extérieur (ci-dessus) paraît assez fermé, uniquement animé par des bandeaux ouverts en parties inférieure et supérieure.

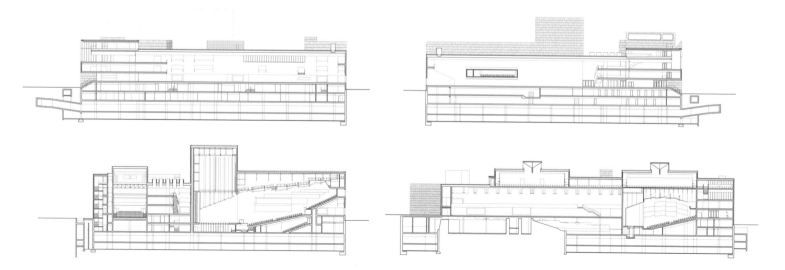

The monolithic appearance of the building is interrupted only by bands of glazing or the occasional larger openings (below).

Das monolithische Erscheinungsbild des Gebäudes wird nur von Glasbändern oder einzelnen größeren Öffnungen unterbrochen (unten).

L'aspect monolithique du bâtiment n'est interrompu que par des bandeaux de verre et quelques grandes baies (ci-dessous).

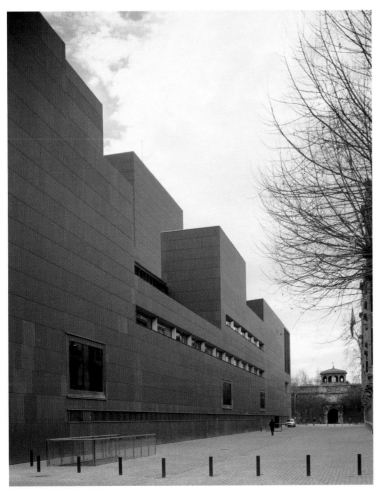

The architects certainly play on the appearance of floating volumes, as is the case in the staircase seen above from two different angles.

Wie bei der oben zu sehenden Treppenanlage spielen die Architekten mit der Idee scheinbar schwebender Baukörper.

Les architectes ont joué sur un principe de volumes suspendus, comme pour cet escalier vu sous deux angles différents.

The rigorous, aligned interior design corresponds closely to the outside appearance of the building, giving it a feeling of coherence not always attained in contemporary architecture.

Die strenge Gestaltung des Innenraums entspricht genau der äußeren Erscheinung des Bauwerks, was dem Ganzen zu einer in der zeitgenössischen Architektur nicht immer vorhandenen Stimmigkeit verhilft.

Les alignements rigoureux des aménagements intérieurs correspondent parfaitement à l'enveloppe extérieure du bâtiment et lui confèrent un sentiment de grande cohérence, parfois absent en architecture contemporaine.

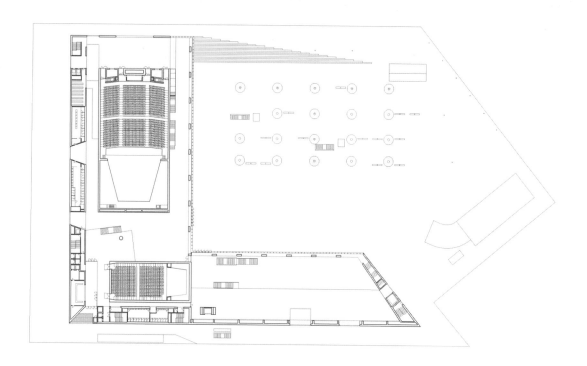

The interior design of auditoriums often escapes the attention of architects involved in such large, complex buildings. In this instance, the rigor displayed both inside and outside the building has been carried into the theater space.

Die Innenarchitektur wird häufig von Architekten, die in derart große, komplexe Projekte eingebunden sind, vernachlässigt. In diesem Fall findet die im Inneren und Äußeren des Gebäudes anzutreffende Strenge auch im Theaterraum ihren Niederschlag.

L'aménagement intérieur de l'auditorium échappe souvent à l'attention des architectes de vastes complexes de ce type. Ici, la rigueur observée à l'extérieur est appliquée au volume intérieur.

MANSILLA + TUÑÓN

**MANSILLA+TUÑÓN
ARQUITECTOS**
Ríos Rosas, 11, 6º
28003 Madrid

Tel/Fax: +34 91 399 30 67
e-mail: circo@circo.e.telefonica.net
Web: www.mansilla-tunon.com

EMILIO TUÑÓN and LUIS MANSILLA were both born in Madrid, respectively in 1958 and 1959, and received their doctorates from the Escuela Técnica Superior de Arquitectura in Madrid (ETSAM) in 1998, creating their firm in Madrid in 1992. They are both full Professors in Architectural Design at ETSAM. In 1993, they created a "thinking exchange cooperative" called Circo with Luis Rojo, and published a bulletin of the same name. Their built projects include: the Archeological and Fine Arts Museum of Zamora (1996); Indoor Swimming Pool in San Fernando de Henares (1998); Fine Arts Museum of Castellón (2001); Auditorium of León (2002); Regional Library and Archive of Madrid (2003); and the MUSAC Contemporary Art Museum in Castilla y León (2002-04), featured here. They won competitions for the urban planning of Valbuena in Logroño and a Public Library in Calle de los Artistas in Madrid in 2003; and for the Town Council of Lalín (2004), and the Helga Alvear Foundation in Cáceres (2005). After being finalists for four Mies van der Rohe Awards (1996, 1998, 2001, and 2003) they have been awarded this price in 2007 for the MUSAC.

MUSAC CONTEMPORARY ART MUSEUM OF CASTILLA Y LEÓN

LEÓN 2002 - 04

CLIENT: Gesturcal S. A.,
Government of Castilla y León
AREA: 10 000 m²
COLLABORATORS: Luis Díaz-Mauriño,
Ainoa Prats, Andrés Regueiro, Jaime Gimeno,
Clara Moneo, Teresa Cruz, Oscar F. Aguayo, Gregory
Peñate, Katrien Vertenten y Ricardo Lorenzana.

Located on the Avenida de los Reyes Leoneses, it is a single-story, 10 000-square-meter building with white concrete walls and large areas of colored glazing. The architects explain that "MUSAC is a new space for culture, regarded as something that visualizes the connections between man and nature. A cluster of chained but independent rooms permit exhibitions of differing sizes and types. Each of the jaggedly shaped rooms constructs a continuous yet spatially differentiated area that opens onto the other rooms and courtyards, providing longitudinal, transversal, and diagonal views. Five hundred prefab beams enclose a series of spaces that feature systematic repetition and formal expressiveness. Outside, the public space takes on a concave shape to hold the activities and encounters, embraced by large colored glass in homage to the city as the place for interpersonal relationships." Cheerful and varied in its appearance, MUSAC certainly takes a different aesthetic approach than many contemporary art museums, where there is an emphasis on a more discreet modernism. But the architects have a ready explanation for this difference. "In contrast to other types of museum spaces that focus on the exhibition of frozen historic collections, MUSAC is a living space that opens its doors to the wide-ranging manifestations of contemporary art," they declare.

An der Avenida de los Reyes Leoneses steht ein 10 000 m² großer einstöckiger Bau mit weiß verputzten Betonwänden und großen farbig verglasten Flächen. Die Architekten erläutern, es handele sich bei „MUSAC um einen neuen Raum für Kultur, der als etwas verstanden wird, das die Verbindungen zwischen Mensch und Natur visualisiert. Eine Gruppe aneinander gereihter, aber unabhängiger Räume ermöglicht Ausstellungen unterschiedlicher Größe und Ausrichtung. Jeder der ungleichmäßig geformten Räume stellt einen fortlaufenden, aber räumlich differenzierten Bereich dar, der sich zu anderen Räumen und Innenhöfen hin öffnet und längs, quer und diagonal gerichtete Ausblicke bietet. 500 vorgefertigte Träger umschließen eine Reihe von Räumen, die sich durch systematische Wiederholung und formale Expressivität auszeichnen. Der Außenraum mit seiner leicht konkaven Form für Aktivitäten und Begegnungen ist eingefasst von großen Flächen farbigen Glases als Reverenz an die Stadt als den Ort zwischenmenschlicher Beziehungen." Das fröhliche, abwechslungsreiche Äußere von MUSAC lässt im Vergleich zu vielen zeitgenössischen Museumsbauten, die von einem dezenteren Modernismus geprägt sind, auf eine andere ästhetische Auffassung schließen. Die Architekten haben allerdings eine Erklärung für diesen Unterschied zur Hand. „Im Gegensatz zu anderen Museen, die sich auf die Ausstellung eingefrorener, historischer Sammlungen konzentrieren, handelt es sich bei MUSAC um einen lebendigen Raum, dessen Türen den breit gefächerten Ausdrucksformen zeitgenössischer Kunst weit offen stehen."

Situé Avenida de los Reyes Leoneses, ce bâtiment de 10 000 m² à murs de béton blanc et vastes plans vitrés de couleur ne comporte qu'un seul niveau. Les architectes expliquent que « le MUSAC est un nouvel espace culturel considéré comme objet visualisant les connexions entre l'homme et la nature. Le regroupement de pièces successives mais indépendantes permet d'exposer des œuvres de types et de dimensions différentes. Chacune de ces salles de forme découpée constitue une zone continue mais spatialement différenciée qui ouvre sur les autres salles et cours, offrant au passant des perspectives longitudinales, transversales et diagonales. Cinq cents poutres préfabriquées délimitent une série d'espaces qui se caractérisent par la répétitivité systématique et l'expressivité formelle. À l'extérieur, l'espace public se présente sous forme d'un espace ovale ouvert aux activités et aux rencontres, entouré d'importants panneaux de verre de couleur conçus en hommage à la ville, lieu par excellence de relations interpersonnelles. » D'aspect chaleureux et varié, le MUSAC répond à une esthétique différente de celle de beaucoup de musées d'art contemporain où l'on privilégie un modernisme plus discret. Les architectes expliquent cette différence : « Par contraste avec d'autres types d'espaces muséaux concentrés sur l'exposition de collections historiques figées, le MUSAC est un espace vivant qui ouvre ses portes à une vaste gamme de manifestations d'art contemporain. »

The use of saturated colors on some surfaces of the building is contrasted with much more neutral, gray facades (below). The shape of the building is relatively complex and unexpected.

Oberflächen mit satten Farben stehen viel neutraleren, grauen Fassaden gegenüber (unten). Die Form des Gebäudes ist relativ komplex und ungewöhnlich.

Les couleurs saturées de certaines parties du bâtiment contrastent avec quelques façades grises (ci-dessous). La forme d'ensemble est relativement complexe et surprenante.

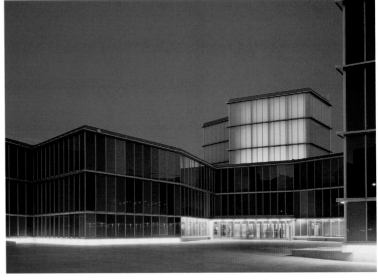

Like a patchwork of bright cloths, the exterior cladding of the building gives little clue of its function, but does convey a sense of positive, bright volumes.

Die wie ein Patchwork aus farbenfrohen Stoffen wirkende Außenseite des Gebäudes lässt kaum Schlüsse auf dessen Funktion zu, vermittelt jedoch den Eindruck positiver, leuchtender Baukörper.

Patchwork de couleurs vives, le parement extérieur ne laisse guère deviner la fonction du bâtiment, mais exprime un sentiment positif.

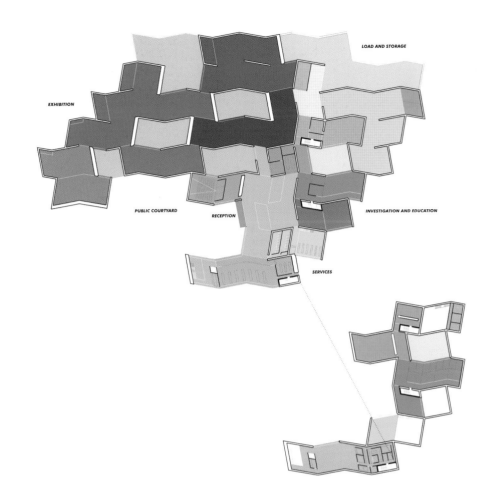

Interior spaces are generous and often carved in powerful forms that allow natural light to penetrate. Overall elevations show that the structure is actually a coherent band with some projecting blocks.

Die großzügig dimensionierten, häufig markant geformten Innenräume lassen Tageslicht einfallen. Aufrisse der Gesamtanlage zeigen, dass es sich um ein fortlaufendes Band mit einigen vorspringenden Blöcken handelt.

Les généreux volumes intérieurs sont souvent sculptés en formes puissantes qui laissent pénétrer la lumière naturelle. Les élévations montrent que le bâtiment est un bandeau cohérent d'où se projettent quelques blocs.

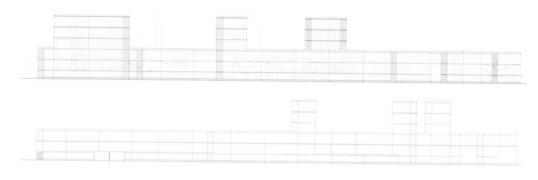

11

FERNANDO MENIS/AMP

FERNANDO MENIS
Puerta Canseco, 35, 2º B
38003 Santa Cruz de Tenerife
Tel: +34 922 28 88 38
Fax: +34 922 15 19 25
e-mail: info@menis.es
Web: www.menis.es

AMP ARQUITECTOS
c/ San José, 2; ático
38001 Santa Cruz de Tenerife
Tel: +34 922 24 51 49
Fax: +34 922 24 71 73
e-mail:
administracion@amparquitectos.com
Web: www.amparquitectos.com

Born in Santa Cruz de Tenerife in 1951, **FERNANDO MENIS** studied architecture in Barcelona, obtaining his degree in 1975 from the Escuela de Arquitectura Superior in Barcelona. He went on to study urban planning in the same school. He worked from 1976 to 1980 on projects such as the Jardin des Halles in Paris, and housing in Marne la Vallée, France. He also worked with the architect Ricardo Fayos in Barcelona (1977). In 1981 he created a firm with **FELIPE ARTENGO RUFINO** and **JOSÉ MARÍA RODRÍGUEZ-PASTRANA MALAGÓN** under the name Artengo, Menis, Pastrana. In 1992 the team turned into a company called Artengo, Menis, Pastrana Arquitectos (AMP Arquitectos, S.L). In 2004 and 2005 Menis, with his new independent studio Menis Arquitectos, won first prize in competitions for the Puerto de la Cruz Harbor, Tenerife; the Cuchillitos de Tristán Park, Tenerife; 55 social-housing units, La Laguna, Tenerife; and for the rehabilitation of the historic center of Agulo and Vallehermoso, La Gomera. His work includes: the MM/MM House, Santa Cruz de Tenerife (1995–98); the Offices of the President of the Government, Santa Cruz de Tenerife (1997–99); 11 bungalows, El Guincho, Tenerife (2000–02); a Swimming Pool on the Spree, Berlin, Germany (2003–04). His Athletics Stadium, Santa Cruz de Tenerife (2002–); and Church of the Holy Redeemer, La Laguna (2004–) are both currently under construction (the first phase of the church is finished and the second began in late 2006).

MAGMA ARTS AND CONGRESS CENTER
ADEJE, TENERIFE
1998-2005

ARCHITECTS: Fernando Martín Menis, Felipe Artengo Rufino,
José María Rodríguez Pastrana
CLIENT: Canarias Congress Bureau Tenerife SUR SA (CCBTS)
AREA: 27 784 m² (site); 20 434 m² (built area)
COST: €28 962 180
COLLABORATORS: Esther Ceballos, Andreas Weihnacht, Ana Salinas
PROJECT MANAGER: Fernando Merino

This convention center for Tenerife is located near the airport and is surrounded by hotels. The architect writes, "The semidesert landscape around it and the presence of the sea are the starting points of the concept of the building. Though it is not situated directly on the water, it does have a strong relation with the ocean, an imposing presence that frames the building with a constant view of La Gomera Island." Thirteen "geometrically shaped" blocks contain program functions such as offices, restrooms, a cafeteria, and so on. "These pieces rise up," explains Menis, "creating a fault line that produces the flow of the roof, imagined as a liquid in motion, outlining the space in every direction. The undulating surface becomes fractured, creating cracks of light and ventilation, splitting and multiplying everywhere with a sensation of lightness." Conference halls are situated between the blocks, with the main room offering 2354 square meters of space, sufficient for 2500 people. This hall can be divided into as many as nine smaller conference rooms if necessary. Menis concludes: "The flowing and undulating role of the roof inside responds to technical necessities which were determined during the construction process, with the help of collaborators, among them the director of the Symphonic Orchestra of Tenerife."

Dieses Kongresszentrum für Teneriffa liegt in der Nähe des Flughafens und ist von Hotels umringt. Der Architekt schreibt: „Die umgebende Halbwüste und die Präsenz des Meeres sind Ausgangspunkte für die Konzeption des Bauwerks. Obgleich es nicht unmittelbar am Wasser liegt, hat es doch eine starke Beziehung zum Meer, das zusammen mit dem unveränderlichen Anblick der Insel La Gomera den Bau auf imposante Weise rahmt." In 13 „geometrisch geformten" Baukörpern sind Funktionen wie Büros, sanitäre Anlagen, eine Cafeteria usw. untergebracht. „Diese Blöcke erheben sich", erklärt Menis, „und schaffen eine Verwerfungslinie, aus der sich das Dach ergießt, das man sich als in Bewegung be-

findliche Flüssigkeit vorstellen muss, die den Raum in jeder Richtung nachzeichnet. Die gewellte Oberfläche bricht, es entstehen Schlitze, durch die Licht und Luft eindringen, sie splittert und schiebt sich mit einer Anmutung von Leichtigkeit übereinander." Zwischen den Blöcken befinden sich Konferenzsäle, von denen der größte eine Fläche von 2354 m² aufweist, ausreichend für 2500 Besucher. Dieser Saal lässt sich bei Bedarf in bis zu neun kleinere Konferenzräume unterteilen. Abschließend fügt Menis hinzu: „Die fließende, gewellte Saaldecke entspricht technischen Anforderungen, die während der Bauzeit mithilfe von Beratern, darunter der Direktor des Sinfonieorchesters von Teneriffa, festgelegt wurden."

Ce centre de congrès pour Tenerife, situé près de l'aeroport, est entouré d'hôtels. Pour l'architecte : « Le paysage environnant semi-désertique et la permanence de l'océan ont été le point de départ du concept de ce bâtiment. Bien qu'il ne s'ouvre pas directement sur l'océan, il possède une relation forte avec celui-ci, son imposante présence qui cadre le bâtiment et la vue omniprésente sur l'île de La Gomera. » Treize blocs « de forme géométrique » contiennent les fonctions définies par le programme comme les bureaux, la cafétéria, etc. « Ces blocs s'élèvent, explique Menis, en créant une ligne de fracture qui provoque le flux de la toiture imaginée comme un liquide en mouvement, et découpent l'espace dans toutes les directions. Cette surface ondulée se fracture, créant des fissures pour la lumière et la ventilation, se fend et se démultiplie en créant une impression de légéreté. Les salles de conférences sont situées entre les blocs. La salle principale de 2354 m² offre 2500 places. Si nécessaire, elle peut se diviser en neuf petites salles. L'architecte conclut : « Le rôle de la toiture fluide et ondulée répond, à l'intérieur, à des contraintes techniques déterminées au cours du processus de construction avec l'assistance de diverses collaborations, dont celle du directeur de l'Orchestre symphonique de Tenerife. »

The folded, strong shapes of the center are certainly closely related to the volcanic history of Tenerife. Rough stone and a twisting plinth look almost as though they had been thrust up out of the earth.

Die gefalteten, prägnanten Formen des Kongresszentrums nehmen Bezug auf die vulkanische Entstehung Teneriffas. Der unbehandelte Stein und eine gewundene Bodenplatte wirken, als habe sie die Erde ausgeworfen.

Les plis puissants, qui caractérisent la forme du Centre, évoquent le passé volcanique de Tenerife. La pierre brute et la plinthe contournée donnent l'impression de jaillir du sol.

The building fits into its environment, but the folding white roof brings a certain lightness to the otherwise massive forms.

Der Bau passt zu seiner Umgebung, aber das gefaltete, weiße Dach fügt den ansonsten wuchtigen Formen eine gewisse Leichtigkeit hinzu.

Le bâtiment est inséré dans son environnement, mais les plis de la toiture blanche insufflent une certaine légèreté dans ces formes par ailleurs massives.

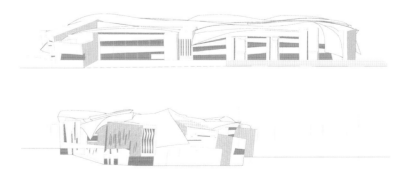

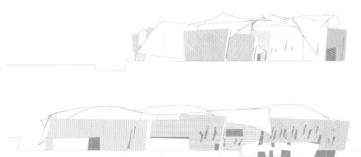

Seen under almost any angle, the stone forms of the center look as though they had been carved out of the living rock of the island.

Aus fast jeder Perspektive wirken die steinernen Formen des Kongresszentrums wie aus dem Gestein der Insel herausgeschnitten.

De presque tous les angles, la pierre qui constitue le Centre donne l'impression d'avoir été directement sculptée dans le rocher.

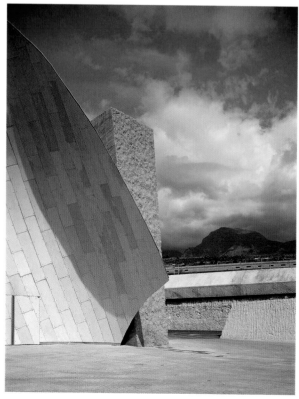

Strong sun makes abrupt shadows play across the stone faces of the building. Certain walls appear to have been cut off, as though they might have originally continued their plunge into the earth.

Starkes Sonnenlicht lässt Schlagschatten über die Fassaden des Bauwerks wandern. Bestimmte Mauern erscheinen abgeschnitten, so als seien sie ursprünglich weiter ins Erdreich vorgedrungen.

Le soleil éclatant génère des ombres abruptes qui jouent sur les façades de pierre. Certains murs semblent avoir été tranchés comme s'ils se poursuivaient dans le sous-sol.

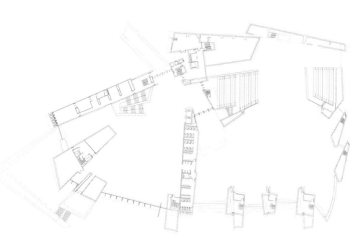

Interior spaces continue the theme of powerful stone surfaces introduced on the exterior of the building. An irregular fan-shaped plan clearly allows for unimpeded functions and for the movement of visitors through the space.

In den Innenräumen wird das im Außenbau eingeführte Thema der machtvollen Steinflächen fortgesetzt. Der unregelmäßige fächerförmige Grundriss lässt sämtliche Funktionen und die ungehinderte Bewegung der Besucher im Raum zu.

Les volumes intérieurs reprennent le thème de la pierre exploité à l'extérieur. Le plan, en forme d'éventail irrégulier, facilite l'implantation des fonctions prévues et le flux des visiteurs.

A plan with folding roof surfaces (below) relates this building to studies carried out on topography or perhaps plate tectonics. Inside, massive stone volumes rise up, as though they had been chiseled out of the volcanic bedrock.

Ein Lageplan mit gefalteten Dachflächen (unten) setzt diese Gebäude in Beziehung zu topografischen Studien oder eventuell zu Plattentektonik. Im Inneren erheben sich mächtige Steinblöcke, so als habe man sie aus dem vulkanischen Fels gemeißelt.

Plan montrant les couvertures à pli (ci-dessous) qui évoquent des études topographiques, ou peut-être la tectonique des plaques. À l'intérieur, s'élèvent des volumes de pierre massifs qui semblent avoir été travaillés dans la roche volcanique.

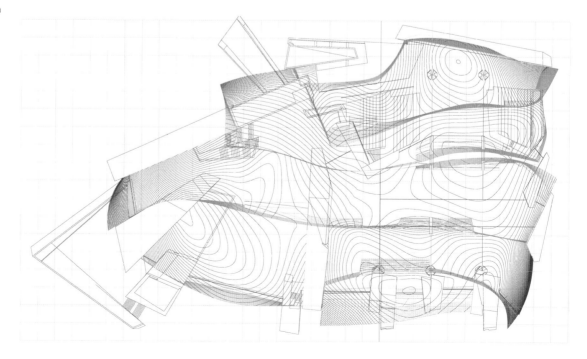

12

MIRALLES TAGLIABUE EMBT

ENRIC MIRALLES - BENEDETTA
TAGLIABUE | EMBT
Passatge de la Pau, 10 Bis, pral.
08002 Barcelona

Tel: +34 93 412 53 42
Fax: +34 93 412 37 18
e-mail: info@mirallestagliabue.com
Web: www.mirallestagliabue.com

Born in Barcelona in 1955, **ENRIC MIRALLES** received his degree from the Escuela Tecnica Superior de Arquitectura in that city in 1978. He died in 2001. He lectured there, at Columbia University in New York, at Harvard, and at the Architectural Association in London. He formed a partnership with Carme Pinós in 1983, and won a competition for the Igualada Cemetery Park on the outskirts of Barcelona in 1985 (completed in 1992). Contrary to the minimalism of other local architects like Viaplana and Piñón with whom he worked from 1974 to 1984, or Estève Bonnel, Miralles was known for the exuberance of his style. While interested in deconstruction as it is applied to literature, Miralles was skeptical about its application to architecture. His work includes: the Morella Boarding School, Castelló (1986-94); the La Mina Civic Center, Barcelona (1987-92); the Huesca Sports Hall (1988-94); and the Olympic Archery Ranges, Barcelona (1989-91). The most visible recent project by the firm was the Scottish Parliament in Edinburgh, Scotland (1998-2004). **BENEDETTA TAGLIABUE** was born in Milan and graduated from the Venice Instituto Universitario di Architettura in 1989. She studied and worked in New York (with Agrest & Gandelsonas) from 1987 to 1989. She worked for Enric Miralles beginning in 1992, first becoming a partner, then leading the studio after his death.

REHABILITATION OF SANTA CATERINA MARKET BARCELONA 1997-2005

CLIENT: Foment de Ciutat Vella S. A.
AREA: Market: 3749 m²; Roof: 5500 m²
PROJECT DIRECTOR: Igor Peraza

Simply put, in the words of the architects, "This building fuses diverse urban functions while interfacing various ages, from past to present, and is symbolized by its pleated roof covered in a colorful tile mosaic that imitates fruit." Some 325 000 hexagonal ceramic tiles in 67 different colors were used for the cladding of the wood-vault and steel beam roof. Three large parallel metal arches with a 42-meter span support the beams. Seizing on the inherent urban complexity of the Ciutat Vella area of Barcelona, the architects have espoused a concept of historic layering. In their words, "We propose a model in which it is not so easy to distinguish between rehabilitation and new construction." The original structure was a Neoclassical building with a metal roof. The new building preserves the original façades and also integrates the newly discovered remains of the Convent of Santa Caterina which had been located on the same site. A large two-level parking lot was also added to the building. The colorful roof pattern can be viewed from nearby buildings, but the original scheme provided for an elevator precisely for that purpose. The elevator has still not been built however. The internal stall pattern is laid out in an irregular plan that recalls some of the firm's other work.

In den Worten der Architekten einfach formuliert, „vereinigt dieses Gebäude unterschiedliche urbane Funktionen, während es verschiedene Zeiten, von der Vergangenheit zur Gegenwart, miteinander koppelt; Sinnbild ist das mit einem Kachelmosaik belegte Faltdach, dessen Farbenpracht an Früchte erinnert." Etwa 325 000 sechseckige Keramikfliesen in 67 verschiedenen Farben wurden für die Verkleidung des aus einem Holzgewölbe und Stahlträgern bestehenden Daches verwendet. Drei große parallele Metallbögen mit einer Spannweite von 42 m stützen die Träger. Anknüpfend an die urbane Komplexität der Altstadt (Ciutat Vella) von Barcelona entschieden sich die Architekten für ein Konzept der historischen Schichtung. Mit anderen Worten: „Wir befürworteten ein Modell, bei dem es nicht leicht fällt, zwischen Sanierung und Neubau zu unterscheiden." Bei dem ursprünglichen Gebäude handelte es sich um einen neoklassizistischen Bau mit einem Metalldach. Das neue Bauwerk bewahrt die ursprüngliche Fassade und integriert darüber hinaus die unlängst entdeckten Reste des Santa-Caterina-Klosters, das am selben Ort gestanden hatte. Außerdem wurde das Gebäude durch ein zweigeschossiges Parkdeck ergänzt. Die farbenprächtige Musterung des Dachs lässt sich von nahegelegenen Gebäuden aus überschauen; zu eben diesem Zweck war in der ursprünglichen Planung ein Fahrstuhl vorgesehen, der allerdings bislang nicht gebaut wurde. Die Verkaufsstände im Inneren sind auf einem unregelmäßigen Grundriss angeordnet, was an einige andere Entwürfe von EMBT erinnert.

Comme l'expliquent très simplement les architectes : « Cette construction fait fusionner des fonctions urbaines diverses, tout en confrontant des périodes variées, du passé au présent. Elle est symbolisée par son toit plissé recouvert d'une mosaïque polychrome en carrelage qui évoque des fruits. » Quelque 325 000 carreaux de céramique hexagonaux de 67 couleurs différentes ont été utilisés pour recouvrir la voûte en bois et acier sous la toiture. Trois grandes arches métalliques parallèles de 42 mètres de portée soutiennent la charpente. Pour s'intégrer à la complexité du quartier de la vieille ville (Ciutat Vella) de Barcelone, les architectes ont opté pour un concept de stratification historique : « Nous proposons un modèle dans lequel il n'est pas si facile de faire la distinction entre réhabilitation et construction neuve. » La structure originelle néo-classique était déjà dotée d'une toiture métallique. Le nouveau bâtiment conserve les façades d'origine et intègre des vestiges récemment redécouverts du couvent de Santa Caterina situé jadis sur le même site. Un vaste parking à deux niveaux a été adjoint au projet. Le motif coloré du toit se voit des immeubles avoisinants, mais le projet de départ prévoyait aussi un ascenseur pour que les passants puissent aussi en profiter. Il n'a pas encore été mis en place pour le moment. La répartition interne des étals se fait selon un plan irrégulier qui rappelle certaines autres interventions de l'agence.

The rolling "tapestry" that covers the rehabili-
tated market brings a note of color or gaiety
to the area, while setting the market apart—
neither fully modern, nor fully from the past.

Das wie ein Bildteppich wirkende gewellte
Dach, das die sanierte Markthalle überdeckt,
bringt Farbe und Fröhlichkeit in das Viertel
und ist gleichzeitig prägendes Merkmal des
Marktes – weder gänzlich modern, noch
gänzlich der Vergangenheit zugehörig.

La « tapisserie » en vague qui recouvre ce
marché réhabilité apporte une note de
couleur et de gaieté dans le quartier tout en
lui assurant une personnalité originale, ni
pleinement moderne, ni pleinement passéiste.

The architects recover the substance of the
space of the old market while making it over
into a modern facility. At the same time, they
do create an aggressively modern intervention on an area that is neither fully traditional
nor specifically recent in design.

Die Architekten bewahren die Substanz des
alten Marktes und verwandeln ihn gleichzeitig
in eine moderne Einrichtung. Außerdem ge-
lingt ihnen eine radikal moderne Intervention
in einem weder durchgehend traditionellen
noch spezifisch modernen Viertel.

Les architectes ont retrouvé la substance
de l'espace de ce marché ancien tout en le
transformant en équipement moderne.
Dans le même temps, ils imposent dans ce
quartier, qui n'est ni vraiment traditionnel
ni spécifiquement récent, une intervention
agressivement moderne.

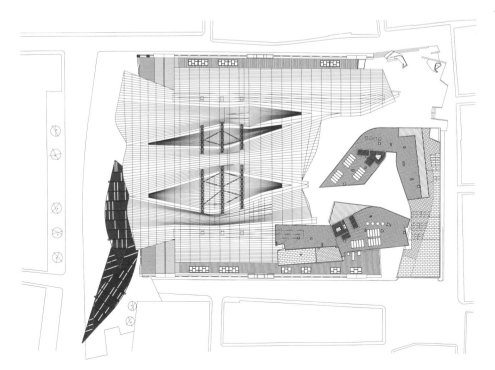

Inside the market, the generous folding shapes make the space agreeable, while an open floor design allows shoppers to circulate freely.

Das Innere der Markthalle wirkt dank der großzügigen gefalteten Formen angenehm, während der stützenfreie Raum die Käufer ungehindert umhergehen lässt.

À l'intérieur, les généreux espaces abrités sous les plis de la toiture créent une atmosphère agréable. Le plan ouvert facilite la libre circulation des clients.

Man war bemüht, der neuen Architektur etwas von der meist mit historischen Bauten assoziierten, komplexen Anmutung zu geben, während das Gebäude gleichwohl modernisiert und auf den neuesten Stand gebracht wurde.

An effort has been made to give the new architecture a feeling of complexity most readily associated with the buildings of the past, while nonetheless modernizing and updating the building.

Les architectes se sont efforcés de donner à leur architecture une impression de complexité généralement plutôt associée aux bâtiments anciens, tout en modernisant et en remettant à niveau les installations.

The floor plan to the right shows the intentional irregularity of the placement of the stalls, together with the curving entry area (lower part of the drawing), all of this within the very regular rectangle that forms the exterior walls.

Auf dem Grundriss rechts sind die bewusst unregelmäßig platzierten Marktstände zu erkennen, im unteren Abschnitt der Zeichnung der geschwungene Eingangsbereich, und all dies innerhalb des von den Außenwänden gebildeten regelmäßigen Rechtecks.

Le plan au sol, à droite, montre l'irrégularité voulue dans l'implantation des étals, et la zone d'entrée incurvée (en bas du plan) contenue à l'intérieur du rectangle strict délimité par les murs extérieurs.

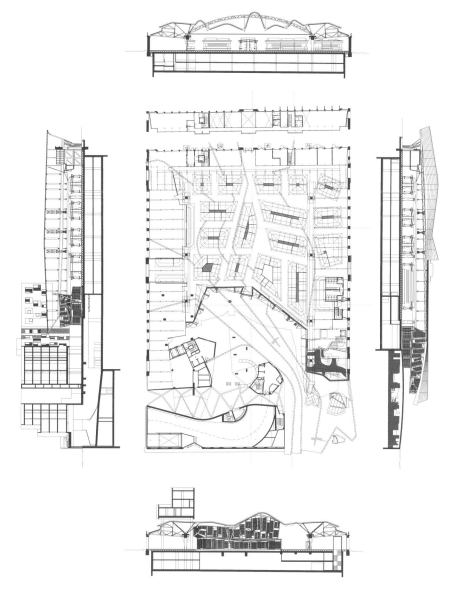

13

RAFAEL MONEO

RAFAEL MONEO
Cinca, 5
28002 Madrid

Tel: +34 91 564 22 57
Fax: +34 91 563 52 17
e-mail: r.moneo@rafaelmoneo.com

RAFAEL MONEO was born in Tudela, Navarra, in 1937. He graduated from the Escuela Técnica Superior de Arquitectura in Madrid (ETSAM) in 1961. The following year, he went to work with Jørn Utzon in Denmark. Rafael Moneo has taught extensively at the ETSAs in Madrid and Barcelona. He was chairman of the Department of Architecture at the Graduate School of Design at Harvard from 1985 to 1990. He won the 1995 Pritzker Prize, and the 2003 RIBA Gold Medal. His work includes: the National Museum of Roman Art, Mérida (1980–86); the San Pablo Airport Terminal in Seville (1989–91) built for Expo '92; Kursaal Auditorium and Congress Center, San Sebastian, Guipuzcoa (1990–99); the Atocha railway station in Madrid (1992); the interior architecture of the Thyssen-Bornemisza Collection in Madrid (1992); the Miró Foundation in Palma (1993); the Davis Museum at Wellesley College, Wellesley, Massachusetts (1993); Potsdamer Platz Hotel and Office Building, Berlin, Germany (1993–98); Murcia Town Hall, Murcia (1995–99); the Cathedral of Our Lady of the Angels, Los Angeles, California (2000–02); an enlargement of the Prado Museum, Madrid (2000–07). He is also working on the Souks in Beirut; the Laboratory for Interface and Engineering at Harvard; the Student Center for the Rhode Island School of Design, Providence, Rhode Island; and the Northwest Science Building at Columbia University in New York. Recent work in Spain includes apartments in Carrer Tres Creus, Sabadell (with José Antonio Martínez Lapeña and Elías Torres, 2000–05); and an extension for the Bank of Spain, Madrid (2001–06).

ART AND NATURE CENTER, BEULAS FOUNDATION
HUESCA 1996 - 2005

CLIENT: Fundación Beulas
AREA: 1677 m²
COST: €4 285 241
COLLABORATORS: Rafael Beneytez,
Peter Carroll, Irene Hwang

The City Council of Huesca, the Government of Aragón and the painter José Beulas, created a foundation for the promotion of contemporary art. The artist and his wife donated a good part of their artistic production, as well as a collection of art by other contemporary artists. The new building by Rafael Moneo is located next to the María Serrate farm, the studio and house of the artist. The adjacent cultivated fields were intentionally maintained in their existing state. Standing in the fields, "The volume dominates the scenery and relates to the nearby ridgelines—as if inspired by the rocky mounds of the *Mallos de Riglos*; it is also encircled by a series of volumes that let one appreciate the powerful scale of the new building," according to the architect. The entry zone is surrounded by the volumes containing a cafeteria, shop, offices, and access to the collections. The permanent exhibition zone at the heart of the building echoes the undulating exterior forms. According to the architect again, "The convex condition of the exterior volume is now transformed into a concave experience defined by the walls and crowned by a radiant ceiling plane. A system of deep beams carrying the glass roof allows for the creation of a 'solar filter' preventing the sun's rays from entering the interior."

Der Stadtrat von Huesca, die Regierung von Aragón und der Maler José Beulas gründeten eine Stiftung zur Förderung der zeitgenössischen Kunst. Der Künstler und seine Frau steuerten einen Gutteil ihres Œuvres sowie eine Sammlung von Werken anderer zeitgenössischer Künstler bei. Das neue Gebäude von Rafael Moneo entstand neben der Farm María Serrate, in der sich Atelier und Wohnung der Künstler befinden. Die angrenzenden Ländereien wurden absichtlich in ihrem vorgefundenen Zustand belassen. Dem Architekten zufolge „beherrscht das in den Feldern stehende Bauwerk die Gegend und nimmt Bezug auf die nahe gelegenen Hügelketten – als wäre es von den felsigen Erhebungen der Mallos de Riglos inspiriert; darüber hinaus ist es von einer Reihe von Baukörpern umgeben, dank derer man sich der mächtigen Erscheinung des neuen Gebäudes

bewusst wird." Im Eingangsareal befinden sich eine Cafeteria, ein Laden, Büros sowie der Zugang zu den Sammlungen. Der im Zentrum des Gebäudes gelegene Bereich der Dauerausstellung nimmt die Wellenform des Gebäudeäußeren auf. Nach Aussage des Architekten „wird hier das von Ausbuchtungen geprägte Äußere in eine von den Wänden definierte konkave Anmutung übertragen, bekrönt von der leuchtenden Deckenfläche. Ein System hoher Balkenträger, die das Glasdach stützen, ermöglichte die Schaffung eines ‚Solarfilters', der die Sonnenstrahlen hindert in den Innenraum einzudringen."

Le conseil municipal d'Huesca, le gouvernement régional de l'Aragón et le peintre José Beulas ont créé une fondation pour la promotion de l'art contemporain. L'artiste et son épouse ont fait donation d'une bonne partie de leur production artistique ainsi que d'une collection de pièces signées d'autres artistes contemporains. Le nouveau bâtiment conçu par Rafael Moneo est adjacent à la ferme María Serrate où habite et travaille Beulas. Les champs cultivés environnants ont été volontairement conservés en l'état. Dressé au milieu des cultures, « le volume domine le paysage et rappelle les lignes de crête voisines – comme inspiré des éminences rocheuses des Mallos de Riglos – mais est également encerclé par une série de volumes qui font apprécier la puissante échelle de la nouvelle construction », explique l'architecte. La zone d'entrée est entourée d'espaces contenant une cafétéria, une boutique, des bureaux et l'accès aux collections. La partie réservée à l'exposition permanente, au cœur du bâtiment, fait écho aux ondulations extérieures. Pour Moneo : « La convexité du volume extérieur se transforme à l'intérieur en une expérience de la concavité définie par les murs et couronnée par le plan radiant du plafond. Un système de poutres soutenant le toit de verre a permis la création d'un « filtre solaire » qui contrôle les rayons solaires pénétrant à l'intérieur. »

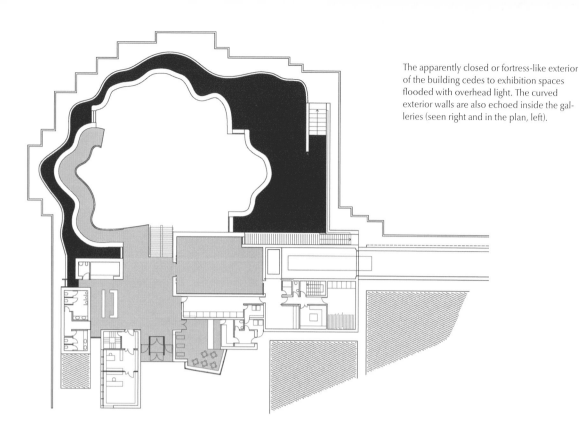

The apparently closed or fortress-like exterior of the building cedes to exhibition spaces flooded with overhead light. The curved exterior walls are also echoed inside the galleries (seen right and in the plan, left).

Das offenbar geschlossene oder festungsgleiche Äußere des Gebäudes wartet in seinem Inneren mit von Oberlichtern erhellten Ausstellungsräumen auf. Wie rechts und im Grundriss links zu erkennen, spiegeln sich die gebogenen Außenmauern in den Galerien wider.

À l'intérieur, l'impression de forteresse fermée cède le pas à des volumes d'exposition baignés de lumière zénithale. Les courbes des murs extérieurs se retrouvent en écho dans les galeries (à droite et sur le plan ci-contre).

NIETO
SOBEJANO

#14

NIETO SOBEJANO
ARQUITECTOS S. L.
c/ Talavera, 4, L-5
28016 Madrid

Tel: +34 91 564 38 30
Fax: +34 91 564 38 36
e-mail: nietosobejano@nietosobe-
jano.com
Web: www.nietosobejano.com

FUENSANTA NIETO and ENRIQUE SOBEJANO graduated as architects from the Escuela Técnica Superior de Arquitec-tura in Madrid (ETSAM) and the Graduate School of Architecture, Planning and Preservation at Columbia University in New York. They are currently teaching at the Universidad Europea in Madrid and at ETSAM, and are the managing partners of Nieto Sobejano Arquitectos S. L. Both have been visiting critics and/or teachers at various Spanish and international universities and institutions, such as the Graduate School of Design at Harvard University; University of Arizona; Technische Universität, Munich; ETSA in Barcelona; University of Turin; University of Stuttgart; UdK Berlin, Germany; University of Cottbus, Germany; Columbia University; the University of Texas, Austin. From 1986 to 1991 they were the editors of the architectural journal *Arquitectura* edited by the Architectural Association of Madrid (Colegio Oficial de Arquitectos de Madrid). Their work has been published in various Spanish and international magazines and books and has been exhibited, amongst other locations, at the Biennale in Venice (2000 and 2002); the Spanish Biennial of Architecture, Seville (2003); "Extreme Eurasia," Tokyo (2005); and "On-Site: New Architecture in Spain," Museum of Modern Art, New York (2006).

AUDITORIUM AND CONFERENCE CENTER
MÉRIDA
2001 · 04

CLIENT: Government of Extremadura, Culture Council
AREA: 10.000 m²
COST: €20 million
COLLABORATORS: Esther Pizarro (Sculptor),
Carlos Ballesteros, Denis Bouvier, Mauro Herrero,
Luis Labrandero, Pedro Quero, Juan Carlos Redondo

"The new building," wrote the architects, "must not only resolve a complex brief to make the music, theatre, and opera uses of the auditorium compatible with the exhibition pavilion. It is also a building with a powerful symbolic presence that, due to its contents and location, will be added to the notable list of modern architecture in Mérida. The Conference Centre is conceived as a massive, unitary piece folded in continuity over itself to define the full and empty spaces that shape a new public zone: a large raised terrace or balcony overlooks the city and the Guadiana River." This terrace is located between the conference and exhibition areas of the complex and can be used independently of either. The main auditorium with its zinc-clad acoustic roof panels seats 1000 persons. The structural framework of the building is made of reinforced concrete, making use of large prefabricated panels. As the architects explain, "Like the *opus incertum* of Roman walls, this heavily textured and pigmented concrete will express a rough, uncertain outer face that contrasts with the metal and glass finish of the two auditorium boxes." Rubber moulds based on a bas-relief sculpture by Esther Pizarro were used to create four basic groups of concrete panels.

„Das neue Gebäude", schrieb der Architekt, „muss nicht nur einen komplexen Bauauftrag so erfüllen, dass die Nutzung des Auditoriums für Musik, Theater und Oper mit dem Ausstellungspavillon kompatibel ist. Es handelt sich außerdem um ein Gebäude von hoher symbolischer Bedeutung, das dank seiner Substanz und seines Standorts in die beachtenswerte Liste moderner Architektur in Mérida aufgenommen wird. Das Kongresszentrum ist als wuchtiger, uniformer Block konzipiert, der gleichsam zusammengefaltet ist, um die geschlossenen und leeren Räume zu definieren, die einen neuen öffentlichen Bereich ergeben: Eine großflächige, erhöhte Terrasse bietet Ausblicke auf die Stadt und den Fluss Guadiana." Diese Terrasse befindet sich zwischen den Konferenz- und Ausstellungsbereichen der Anlage und kann von beiden unabhängig genutzt werden. Das Hauptaudi-torium mit seinen verzinkten, schallabsorbierenden Dachplatten bietet 1000 Personen Platz. Das konstruktive Tragwerk des Gebäudes, für das große, vorgefertigte Platten verwendet wurden, besteht aus Stahlbeton. Dazu führen die Architekten aus: „Wie das ‚opus incertum' der römischen Mauern wird dieser stark strukturierte und pigmentierte Beton eine raue, unbestimmte Außenansicht ergeben, die mit der aus Metall und Glas bestehenden Haut der beiden eingeschobenen ‚Auditoriumskästen' kontrastiert." Eine Flachreliefskulptur von Esther Pizarro lieferte die Vorlagen für Gussformen aus Gummi, mit denen man vier grundlegende Typen von Betonplatten anfertigte.

« Ce nouveau bâtiment, écrivent les architectes, devait apporter une solution à un programme complexe qui spécifiait un auditorium utilisable aussi bien pour la musique, le théâtre ou l'opéra, et compatible avec le pavillon d'expositions. Mais en plus, ce devait être un bâtiment à forte présence symbolique qui, du fait de son contenu et de sa situation, enrichirait le remarquable patrimoine d'œuvres d'architecture moderne à Mérida. Le centre de conférences est un élément massif et unitaire replié sur lui-même pour définir des espaces pleins ou vides qui permettent d'ouvrir une nouvelle zone au public telle une vaste terrasse surélevée ou balcon qui donne sur la ville et la Guadiana. » Cette terrasse située entre les zones de conférences et d'expositions peut servir indifféremment à l'une ou à l'autre. L'auditorium principal habillé de panneaux de couverture acoustiques recouverts de zinc peut recevoir 1000 personnes. L'ossature du bâtiment est en béton armé et fait appel à de grands panneaux préfabriqués. L'architecte ajoute en précisant : « Comme dans le cas de l'*opus incertum* des Romains, ce béton lourdement texturé et pigmenté exprimera une présence extérieure brute et peu définie contrastant avec les finitions en métal et en verre des deux « boîtes » des auditoriums. » Des moules en caoutchouc réalisés d'après une sculpture en bas-relief d'Esther Pizarro ont servi à créer quatre types de panneaux de béton.

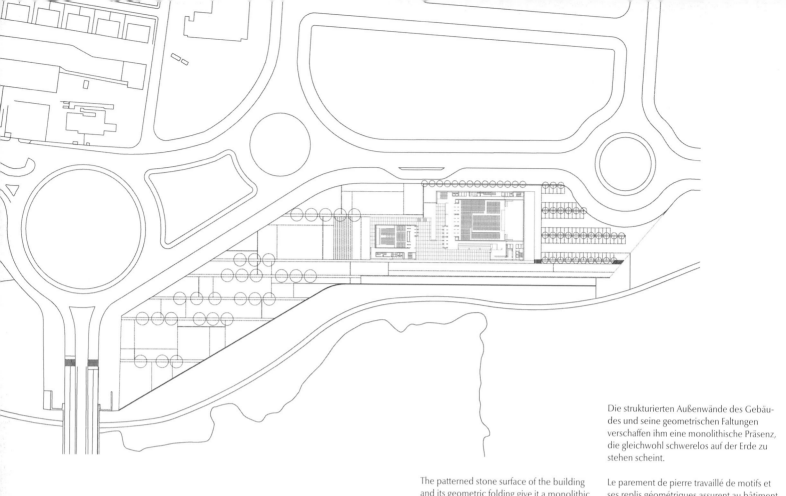

Die strukturierten Außenwände des Gebäudes und seine geometrischen Faltungen verschaffen ihm eine monolithische Präsenz, die gleichwohl schwerelos auf der Erde zu stehen scheint.

The patterned stone surface of the building and its geometric folding give it a monolithic presence, which seems nonetheless to sit lightly on the earth.

Le parement de pierre travaillé de motifs et ses replis géométriques assurent au bâtiment une présence monolithique, même s'il semble ne reposer qu'à peine sur le sol.

A section of the building and an image of its profile (above) show how the apparent simplicity of the form results in a practical facility—an example of the inventiveness of contemporary Spanish architecture.

Ein Schnitt und das Profil des Gebäudes zeigen, wie die offenkundige Schlichtheit der Form eine praktische Einrichtung ergibt – ein Beispiel für den Ideenreichtum der zeitgenössischen spanischen Architektur.

Une coupe et le profil du bâtiment (ci-dessus) montrent comment l'apparente simplicité de la forme aboutit à des installations de sens pratique – un exemple de l'esprit inventif de l'architecture espagnole contemporaine.

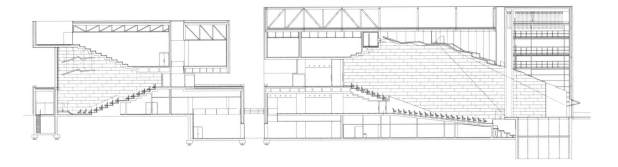

The strongly formed stone blocks of the building rise up, appearing almost to float or to create an impossibly long cantilever, revealing the internal light of the center at night.

Die markant geformten Steinblöcke des Bauwerks erheben sich, um fast schwebend unglaublich lang gezogene Überhänge zu bilden, die bei Nacht die Innenbeleuchtung erkennen lassen.

De puissants blocs de pierre se dressent, paraissent presque flotter ou décrivent des porte-à-faux incroyablement longs que souligne l'éclairage nocturne interne.

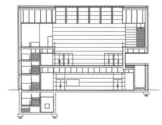

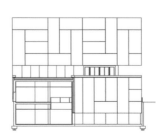

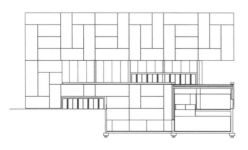

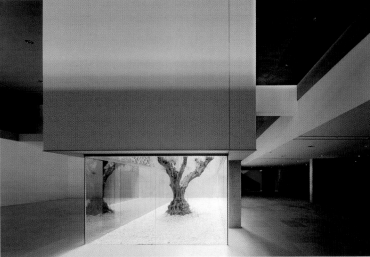

The use of further floating forms, and the rigorous outline of the auditorium demonstrate the overall coherence of the design, from the inside out.

Weitere scheinbar schwebende Elemente und die strengen Konturen des Auditoriums veranschaulichen die von innen nach außen reichende Stimmigkeit des Entwurfs.

La présence répétée de ces blocs en suspension et le dessin rigoureux de l'auditorium illustrent la cohérence d'ensemble du projet entre l'intérieur et l'extérieur.

15

PAREDES
PEDROSA

PAREDES PEDROSA
ARQUITECTOS
c/ Nervión, 12
28002 Madrid

Tel/Fax: +34 91 411 20 17
e-mail: estudio@paredespedrosa.com
Web: www.paredespedrosa.com

IGNACIO GARCÍA PEDROSA was born in Madrid in 1957. He graduated from the Escuela Técnica Superior de Arquitectura in Madrid (ETSAM) in 1983, and has taught Project Design there since 1995. He has also been an Invited Professor at ETSA in Pamplona. ÁNGELA GARCÍA DE PAREDES was born in Madrid in 1958. She graduated from ETSAM in 1982, and has been a Guest Professor at the Barcelona ETSA and Pamplona ETSA. They have also taught in Rome, Mexico, Munster, Santo Domingo, Buenos Aires, at the City University of New York (CCNY) and at the Polytechnic of Milan, Italy. They created their firm in Madrid in 1990. Their recent work includes: a Public Library in Madrid (2001–03); Auditorium and Congress Center, Peñíscola (2002–03), featured here; Archaeology Museum, Almería (2000–04); Faculty of Psychology, Madrid (2003–04); Torner Museum, Cuenca (2004–05); Olimpia Theater, Madrid (2002–05); and social housing in Madrid (2004–06). Currently under construction: Olmeda Roman Villa Museum, Palencia (2005–07); Public Library in Madrid (2006–08); and Bodegas Real wine cellar, Valdepeñas (2004–08).

AUDITORIUM AND CONVENTION CENTER
PEÑÍSCOLA
2003

CLIENT: Proyecto Cultural de Castellón, S.A.
Government of Valencia
COST: €12 328 610
AREA: 6175 m²
COLLABORATORS: Eva M. Neila,
Silvia Colmenares, Javier Arpa
SITE ARCHITECTS: Jaime Prior,
Ramón Monfort

The program for this project includes a music hall and cinema with 702 seats, an exhibition gallery, three meeting rooms with 70 seats each, a cafeteria, dressing rooms, offices, and storage space. A white, undulating concrete ceiling and wood finishing mark the main hall. The architects explain, "The location of the site nearby Peñíscola Castle, a National Heritage Monument, and a park, in front of the Mediterranean, determined our proposal. Our will was to link all inner spaces to the park and to the sea in front of it. Therefore, the building displays an open, fragmented front toward the park, allowing views of the sea from the upper level and letting the former penetrate through the outer plaza. Meanwhile, the rest of the perimeter isolates the structure from the surroundings." A loggia at the entrance to the building provides a public meeting area that links to the park. The wave pattern of the roof, covered with zinc, is visible from the castle. The architects conclude, "The entrance hall is understood as a fluid space that links all independent areas of the building. The ground floor hosts the main room, administration areas, and the exhibition room. Above, three congress rooms, the press hall, and the cafeteria are located. The latter opens up as a viewpoint toward the sea."

Dieses Projekt umfasst eine auch als Kino genutzte Konzerthalle mit 702 Plätzen, eine Kunstgalerie, drei Sitzungssäle mit jeweils 70 Plätzen, eine Cafeteria, Umkleideräume, Büros und Lagerraum. Eine weiß verputzte, wellenförmige Decke und mit Holz verschalte Wände kennzeichnen den Hauptsaal. Die Architekten erklären: „Die Lage des Baugeländes nahe dem Schloss von Peñíscola, einem Baudenkmal von nationaler Bedeutung, und einem Park am Mittelmeer war maßgeblich für unsere Planung. Wir wollten alle Innenräume in Verbindung mit dem Park und dem davorliegenden Meer bringen. Deshalb wendet der Bau dem Park eine offene, fragmentierte Fassade zu, die von der oberen Ebene Ausblicke auf das Meer ermöglicht, das auch die äußere Platzanlage erreicht. Dagegen schirmt die übrige Umfassung das Gebäude von der Umgebung ab." Eine Loggia am Gebäudeeingang dient den Besuchern als Treffpunkt, der Zugang zum Park bietet. Vom Schloss aus ist das wellenförmige, mit Zink verkleidete Dach zu sehen. Die Architekten schließen mit der Bemerkung: „Die Eingangshalle ist als Raum zu verstehen, der sämtliche Bereiche des Gebäudes miteinander verbindet. Im Erdgeschoss befinden sich der Hauptsaal, Verwaltungsbüros sowie der Ausstellungsraum. Auf der darüber liegenden Ebene finden drei Konferenzräume, die Pressehalle und eine Cafeteria Platz, von der sich Ausblicke aufs Meer bieten."

Le programme comprenait une salle de cinéma et de musique de 702 places, une galerie d'expositions, trois salles de réunions de 70 places chacune, une cafétéria, des vestiaires, des bureaux et des espaces de stockage. Un plafond en béton ondulé blanc et des habillages en bois confèrent à la salle principale de la personnalité. Selon l'architecte : « La présence, non loin du site, du château de Peñíscola, monument classé, et d'un parc en bordure de la Méditerranée, a déterminé notre proposition. Notre volonté était de créer des liens entre tous les espaces intérieurs, le parc et la mer... C'est pourquoi le bâtiment présente une façade ouverte et fragmentée vers le parc qui offre, au niveau supérieur, des vues sur la mer, et se laisse pénétrer par le parc au niveau de la place (plaza). Mais le reste du périmètre isole néanmoins la structure de son environnement. » À l'entrée, une loggia peut servir de lieu de rencontre relié au parc. Le toit en vague recouvert de zinc est visible du château. Les architectes concluent en précisant : « Le hall d'entrée est un espace fluide qui relie toutes les zones indépendantes du bâtiment. Le rez-de-chaussée abrite la salle principale, les locaux administratifs et la salle d'expositions. Au-dessus se trouvent trois salles de réunions, la salle de presse et la cafétéria. Cette dernière offre un point de vue sur la mer. »

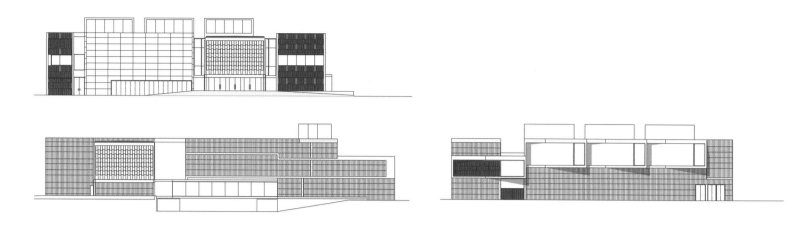

This overall façade view shows the architects' intentional variation of façade treatments, ranging from an open framework on the right to a blank, undulating wall in the middle, where the words "Palau de Congressos" are carved.

Diese Gesamtansicht der Fassade zeigt die von den Architekten intendierte vielfältige Gestaltung, die von offenem Rahmenwerk rechts zu einer glatten, gebogenen Wand in der Mitte reicht, in die die Worte „Palau de Congressos" eingemeißelt wurden.

Cette vue d'ensemble de la façade montre les variations de traitement apportées par l'architecte, entre une ossature totalement ouverte à droite et le mur aveugle du centre sur lequel sont gravés les mots « Palau de Congressos ».

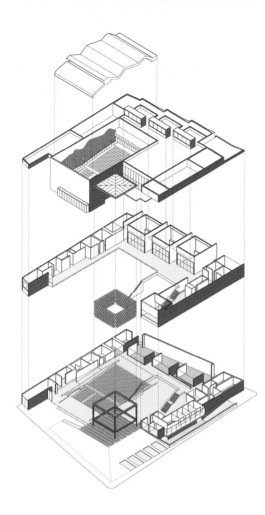

The architecture offers an orchestrated variety of openings and uses of space and volume, including the basketwork box, lifted up on pilotis (right).

Die Architektur zeichnet sich durch eine inszenierte Vielfalt von Öffnungen, Räumen und Volumen aus, darunter das auf Stützen angehobene Flechtwerk (rechts).

L'architecture se distingue par l'orchestration d'un grand nombre d'ouvertures et différentes utilisations de l'espace et du volume comme ici avec cette immense boîte en vannerie montée sur pilotis (à droite).

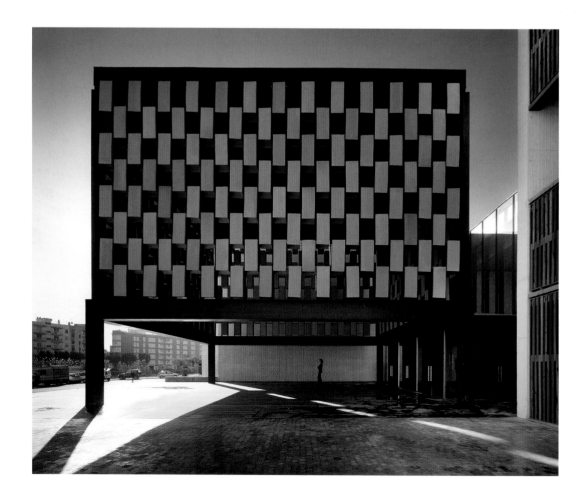

The varied façades visible on pages 164–165 can be discerned at the top of the site plan (below). The auditorium is rigorous but gives an impression of floating weightiness.

Die auf den Seiten 164–165 zu sehenden unterschiedlichen Fassaden erscheinen auch oben auf dem Lageplan (unten). Das Auditorium wirkt kompromisslos, erweckt gleichwohl aber den Eindruck schwebender Schwerelosigkeit.

Les différentes façades visibles sur les pages 164–165 figurent en haut du plan d'ensemble (ci-dessous). La rigueur de dessin de l'auditorium laisse une impression de poids suspendu.

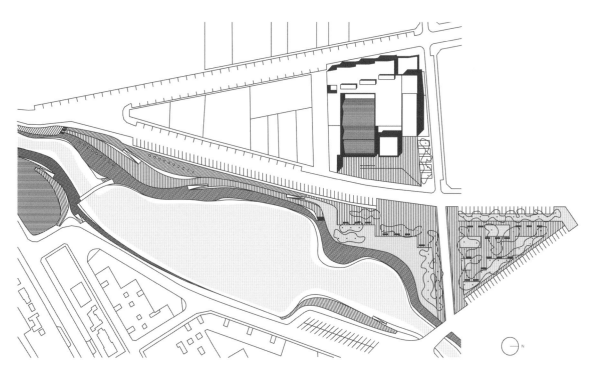

#16

RCR
ARQUITECTES

RCR ARANDA PIGEM
VILALTA ARQUITECTES
Passeig de Blay, 34, 2º
17800 Olot (Girona)

Tel: +34 972 26 91 05
Fax: +34 972 26 75 58
e-mail: rcr@rcrarquitectes.es
Web: www.rcrarquitectes.es

RAFAEL ARANDA, CARME PIGEM and RAMON VILALTA completed their studies in architecture at the Escuela Técnica Superior de Arquitectura of Vallés (ETSAV) in 1987, and the following year created their own studio, RCR Arquitectes, in Olot, the city where they were born. Since 1989 they have been Consultant Architects for the Natural Park in the Volcanic Zone of La Garrotxa. They have taught Urbanism (1989–2001, Vilalta) and Studio Projects (1992–2003, Pigem) at ETSAV. Pigem was a Guest Lecturer at the Department of Architecture at the Swiss Federal Institute of Technology (ETHZ). They have won a number of competitions ranging from a Lighthouse in Punta Aldea in 1988 to the Crematorium of Hofheide, Belgium.

M-LIDIA HOUSE
MONTAGUT
2001 - 02

CLIENT: not disclosed
COST: €168 500
AREA: 170 m²
COLLABORATORS: M. Subiras, A. Sáez,
A. Planagumà, M. Sánchez

The architects explain that this house is located in "an insipid development with good views, a simple brief for a young couple with a small budget." They go on to explain: "Workshop-built, this is a box with thin walls and glass protected by metal mesh that opens outwards and creates clefts that conquer the air. The box rests on walls that configure a half-buried area that contains the garage. The interior space is attached to the thick or the thin wall, if we consider its section with all of the services clustered together, and it is either tripartite or single space, depending on how we position the glass enclosures of the cleft that change the perception of the space in terms of its dimensions and the full/empty relationship, with interior/exterior qualities."

Die Architekten erläutern, dieses Haus liege „in einer gesichtslosen Siedlung mit guten Ausblicken, ein einfacher Auftrag für ein junges Paar mit kleinem Budget." Weiterhin führen sie aus, es handle sich bei dieser „Werkstattmontage um einen Kasten mit dünnen Wänden und von Drahtgeflecht geschütztem Glas, der sich nach außen öffnet und Spalten bildet, in denen sich die Luft fängt. Der Kasten steht auf Mauern, die ein abgesenktes Areal umgeben, das die Garage enthält. Der Innenraum grenzt an die dicke oder die dünne Wand, wenn wir seine

Durchdringung sämtlicher dort versammelter Funktionen in Betracht ziehen; außerdem ist er entweder dreigeteilt oder einräumig, je nachdem wie wir die gläsernen Umhüllungen der Spalte positionieren, die die Wahrnehmung des Raums hinsichtlich seiner Dimensionen verändern sowie das Verhältnis von voll und leer zur inneren und äußeren Beschaffenheit."

Les architectes présentent ainsi le problème posé par « un lotissement insipide mais avec une belle vue, un programme simple pour un jeune couple mais un petit budget ». Ils poursuivent en expliquant qu'« il s'agit d'une boîte aux murs minces et aux parois de verre de construction artisanale, protégée par un fin treillis métallique qui s'ouvre vers l'extérieur en formant des crevasses qui génèrent un appel d'air. La boîte repose sur des murs qui configurent une zone semi-enterrée contenant le garage. Le volume intérieur déterminé par un mur épais ou mince, vu en coupe, regroupe tous les services et constitue un espace tantôt tripartite tantôt unique, selon la manière dont on organise la clôture de verre de la crevasse, ce qui modifie la perception de l'espace en termes de dimensions et de relation plein/vide, par la modification du rapport intérieur / extérieur. »

The closed boxes of the house (above) resemble shipping containers, albeit in a more sophisticated and carefully crafted form. Glass surfaces or opening louvers bring ample light into the house.

Die geschlossenen Kästen des Gebäudes (oben) ähneln Schiffscontainern, wenngleich in anspruchsvoller, sorgfältig gefertigter Form. Glasflächen oder zu öffnende Lamellen lassen reichlich Licht in das Innere.

Les boîtes fermées qui constituent la maison (ci-dessus) ressemblent à des conteneurs d'expédition, bien que traitées avec plus de sophistication, bien sûr. Les plans vitrés ou des ouvertures à persiennes éclairent généreusement l'intérieur de la maison.

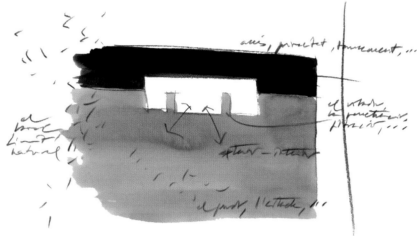

A sketch, above, shows the overall form as being an accumulation of rectangular boxes closing out most of their environment, perhaps ready to be hauled away when the owner desires.

Auf der oben zu sehenden Skizze stellt sich die Gesamtform als Ansammlung von rechteckigen Kästen dar, die sich gegen ihre Umgebung weitgehend abschotten, vielleicht bereit auf Wunsch ihres Eigners abtransportiert zu werden.

Le croquis ci-dessus montre que le plan d'ensemble se compose d'une accumulation de boîtes rectangulaires fermées sur l'environnement, attendant peut-être le désir du propriétaire de les transporter ailleurs.

The notched openings in the house open toward a green space, and furniture is kept to a strict minimum, as can be seen from the two images at the top of these pages.

Die in das Haus eingeschnittenen Öffnungen tun sich zu einer Grünfläche auf; wie auf den beiden Abbildungen oben auf der Seite zu sehen, beschränkt sich die Möblierung auf ein absolutes Minimum.

Les ouvertures découpées dans les murs donnent sur un espace vert. Le mobilier est réduit au minimum comme on peut le voir sur les deux photos du haut de ces pages.

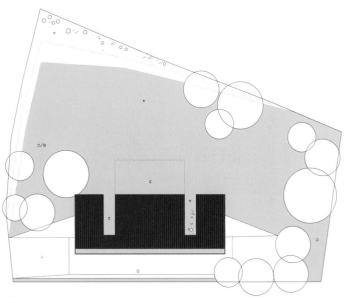

Sections of the house show that despite appearances it consists only in a series of boxes laid on the earth; the visible volumes are in fact set on a half-buried area that contains the garage.

Schnitte des Hauses zeigen, dass es ungeachtet des äußeren Scheins nur aus einer Reihe von auf dem Boden stehenden Kästen besteht; die sichtbaren Baukörper stehen auf einem halb unter Planum liegenden Areal, das die Garage enthält.

Les différentes coupes de la maison montrent que malgré les apparences, elle est constituée d'une succession de boîtes posées à même le sol ; les volumes extérieurs reposent en fait sur une zone à moitié enterrée qui contient le garage.

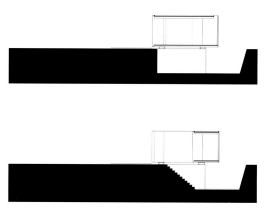

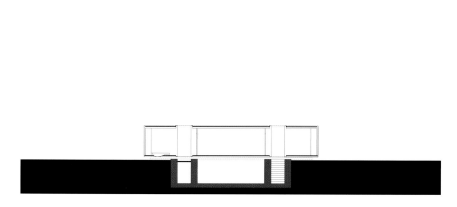

ELS COLORS KINDERGARTEN
MANLLEU 2003 - 04

CLIENT: Manlleu Town Hall
COST: €811 023
AREA: 928 m²
COLLABORATORS: M. Tapies,
Blázquez-Guanter, M. Subiras, M. Linares,
J. Torrents, G. Rodriguez, M. Braga, F. Spratley

This colorful kindergarten, with red, orange, and yellow glass, is intended for very small children, up to three years of age only. In fact, color and the way it is perceived by small children is an important part of this design. The architects write, "In a construction game, the form is threaded together on the basis of the juxtaposition and overlapping of simple pieces. The ease of composition derives from the uniform size of these pieces, and the final identification of each one, which now form a single unit, is derived from color. A child's perception of space is different; their point of view is much lower than an adult's, and the erect head perceives different perspectives that extend the relative dimensions. Facilitating orientation and location for children under the age of three is a spatial learning task that is important in their process of gaining independence and confidence. The open, fluid nature of the materialization of the boundaries contributes to their experience of relations instead of self-absorption."

Dieses farbenfrohe Kindergartengebaude mit rotem, orangefarbenem und gelbem Glas ist fur Kleinkinder bis zu drei Jahren gedacht. Tatsächlich machen die Farben und die Art, wie sie von kleinen Kindern wahrgenommen werden, einen wichtigen Teil dieses Entwurfs aus. Die Architekten schreiben dazu: „In einem Baukasten entsteht die Form auf der Basis des Nebeneinanders oder Überschneidens einfacher Teile. Die Leichtigkeit der Komposition beruht auf der einheitlichen Größe der Teile und die endgültige Bestimmung all dieser Teile, die eine Einheit bilden, ist von der Farbe abgeleitet. Ein Kind nimmt Raum anders wahr; sein Blick-

punkt liegt viel tiefer als der eines Erwachsenen und der erhobene Kopf nimmt andere Perspektiven wahr, die die relativen Dimensionen erweitern. Um Kindern unter drei Jahren die Orientierung und das Auffinden zu erleichtern, muss man ihnen räumliche Aufgaben stellen, die wichtig sind für den Erwerb von Unabhängigkeit und Selbstvertrauen. Der offene, fließende Charakter der materiellen Gestaltung der Begrenzungen fordert ihre Erfahrung von Beziehungen statt einen Rückzug auf sich selbst zu bestärken."

Cette crèche polychrome aux murs de verre rouge, orange et jaune a été conçue pour de très jeunes enfants (jusqu'à 3 ans). La couleur et la façon dont elle est perçue par eux sont des éléments importants du projet. Pour l'architecte : « Dans un jeu de construction, la forme s'élabore à partir de la juxtaposition et de la superposition d'éléments simples. La facilité de composition tient aux dimensions uniformes de ces pièces. L'identification finale de chacune d'entre elles, qui constituent maintenant une composition unique, est issue de la couleur. La perception de l'espace par un enfant est différente de la nôtre. Son point de vue est beaucoup plus bas que celui d'un adulte, et sa tête levée perçoit des perspectives différentes qui acroissent les dimensions relatives. Faciliter l'orientation et la localisation spatiale des enfants de moins de 3 ans leur permet d'apprendre l'espace, tâche importante dans leur processus d'indépendance et de confiance en soi. La nature fluide et ouverte de la matérialisation des limites contribue à leur expérience des relations entre les choses; à l'opposé de leur absorption par elles. »

The architects combine a rigorously geometric plan and design with bright colors and shapes that are intended to appeal to children.

Die Architekten kombinieren einen streng geometrischen Grundriss mit satten Farben und Formen, die Kinder anregen sollen.

Les architectes ont combiné un plan de formes géométriques rigoureuses à des couleurs vives censées plaire aux enfants.

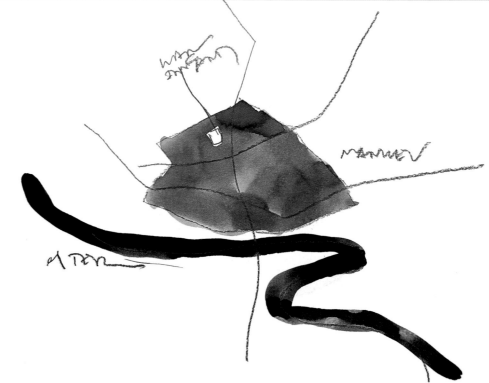

The boxes that form the kindergarten again seem to sit on the earth, almost unattached to the site, though trees are reflected in its surface.

Die Kästen, aus denen der Kindergarten besteht, scheinen fast ohne Bindung zum Baugrund auf dem Boden zu stehen, wenngleich sich Bäume in den Fassaden spiegeln.

Les « boîtes » qui constituent la crèche semblent à peine appuyées sur le sol, presque sans lien avec lui, même si des arbres se reflètent sur ses façades.

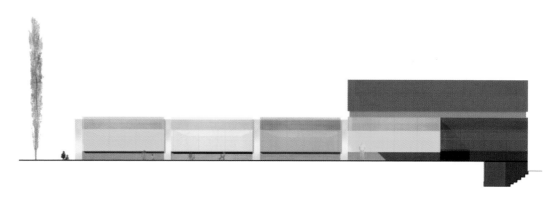

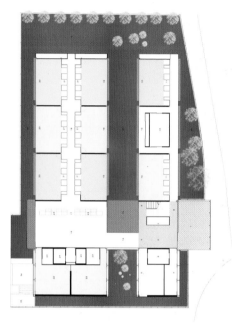

The strictly rectangular plan is no indication of a lack of imagination—the architects prefer to create surprises within these geometric confines, sometimes with floor-to-ceiling glass walls.

Der streng rechtwinklige Grundriss ist kein Anzeichen für mangelnde Fantasie – den Architekten gefällt es, innerhalb dieser geometrischen Grenze für Überraschungen zu sorgen, bisweilen mit deckenhohen Glaswänden.

Le plan n'est pas strictement orthogonal par manque d'imagination. Les architectes ont préféré créer des surprises dans les limites de ce cadre géométrique, par des murs vitrés tout en hauteur par exemple.

Within what can only be called a modernist plan, the architects have created an open, pleasant environment on a human scale, where children can clearly feel at ease.

Im Rahmen eines zweifellos modernistischen Projekts schufen die Architekten ein offenes, angenehmes Umfeld in menschlichem Maßstab, in dem sich Kinder wohl fühlen können.

Grâce à ce plan résolument moderniste, les architectes ont créé un environnement ouvert et agréable, à échelle humaine, dans lequel les enfants peuvent se sentir à l'aise.

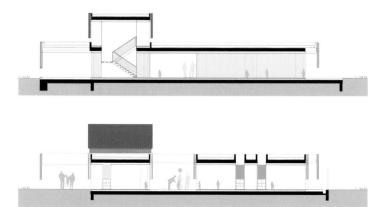

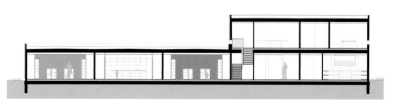

The use of ample glazing, often in the form of floor-to-ceiling glazing as in the glass corridors seen here, is an unexpected feature of the design, contributing to an openness that may also be useful in the observation of the children.

Die großzügige Verwendung von Glas, häufig in Form deckenhoher Verglasung wie bei den hier abgebildeten gläsernen Korridoren, ist ein unerwartetes Merkmal des Entwurfs, das zu der eventuell auch für die Beaufsichtigung der Kinder nützlichen Offenheit beiträgt.

Le recours aux parois vitrées, souvent toute hauteur comme dans les corridors vitrés, est un élément inattendu de ce projet. Il confirme le sentiment d'ouverture, mais peut aussi se révéler utile pour surveiller les enfants.

17

SELGAS
CANO

**JOSÉ SELGAS Y LUCIA CANO
ARQUITECTOS**
Avenida Casaquemada, 1, 1º
28023 Madrid (La Florida)

Tel: +34 91 307 64 81
e-mail: selgas1@selgascano.com
Web: www.selgascano.com

JOSÉ SELGAS was born in Madrid in 1965. He got his architecture degree at the Escuela Técnica Superior de Arquitectura in Madrid (ETSAM) in 1992. He worked with Francesco Venecia in Naples (1994–95). **LUCIA CANO** was also born in Madrid in 1965, and received her degree from ETSAM in 1992. She worked with Julio Cano Lasso from 1997 to 2003. They have won a number of first prize awards in competitions, including: Ideas Competition for Social Housing (Madrid, 1993); the competition for the Badajoz Center published here (1999); for the Cartagena Conference and Auditorium (2001, under construction); for a similar facility in Plasencia (2005, under construction). They also participated in the "On-Site: New Architecture in Spain" exhibition at the Museum of Modern Art, New York (2006). The architects are presently completing the construction of 20 garden villas in Vallecas, Madrid.

CONFERENCE CENTER AND AUDITORIUM
BADAJOZ
1999 - 2006

CLIENT: Government of Extremadura
AREA: 15 000 m²
COST: €22 million
COLLABORATORS: Lara Resco, José de Villar, Talia Dombriz, Paula Rosales, Blas Anton, César G.ª Guerra, Ángel Azagra, Miguel San Millán, Manuel Cifuentes, Carlos Chacón, Brigitte Hollega, Mara Sánchez, Juan Bueno, Fabián Fdez. de Alarcón

Built in an old circular bullring which in its turn was inserted into a 17th-century pentagonal Vauban bastion, this round building has a central void measuring 75 meters in diameter. The architects explain that although it was difficult to work with this site, they feel that they succeeded in revealing what was originally present even as they built anew. This is in particular the case of the central void, whose function they in a sense inverted—bringing the public into the space formerly reserved for the bulls. The circular form of the void is covered with polyester rings intended to make the limits of the space dissolve in the light. The actual building is a concrete and steel design with fiberglass and polyester profiles on the exterior rings, 12-cm white Plexiglas tubes on the main cylinder and polycarbonate boards on the main auditorium walls and ceiling. They explain that this "magic trick"— making the void indeterminate—is only possible because they have placed a good part of the programmatic requirements of the project below grade. The interior is dealt with in a similar fashion, with translucent materials and a central oculus that brings light into the middle of the building. The architects conclude that the more they worked on the lightness and transparency of the building, the more they came to assume the heritage of this very particular site.

In eine alte, kreisförmige Stierkampfarena, die man ihrerseits in eine fünfeckige Bastion Vaubans aus dem 17. Jahrhundert eingesetzt hatte, verfügt dieser Rundbau über einen zentralen Raum mit einem Durchmesser von 75 m. Die Architekten erklären, dass es ihnen ihrer Ansicht nach trotz der schwierigen Bedingungen an diesem Ort gelungen ist, das hier ursprünglich Vorhandene zu zeigen, obwohl sie etwas Neues schufen. Das trifft insbesondere für den zentralen Platz zu, dessen Funktion sie in gewisser Hinsicht umkehrten, indem sie das Publikum in den vormals den Stieren vorbehaltenen Bereich bringen. Der kreisrunde Platz ist mit Ringen aus Polyester bedeckt, die bewirken sollen, dass sich die Grenzen des Raums in Licht auflösen. Das eigentliche Gebäude besteht aus Beton und Stahl mit Profilen aus Fiberglas und Polyester auf den äußeren Ringen, weißen Plexiglas-röhren mit 12 cm Durchmesser auf dem Hauptzylinder und Polycarbonatverschalung an den Wänden und der Decke des Hauptauditoriums. Sie erklären, dieser „magische Trick", den inneren Raum unendlich erscheinen zu lassen, funktioniere nur, weil sie einen Gutteil der programmatischen Anforderungen dieses Projekts unter die Erde verlegten. Mit lichtdurchlässigen Materialien und einem zentralen Oberlicht brachten sie Helligkeit in die Mitte des Gebäudes. Abschließend bemerken die Architekten, dass sie sich das Erbe dieses ganz besonderen Ortes umso nachhaltiger aneigneten, je mehr sie an der Leichtigkeit und Transparenz des Gebäudes arbeiteten.

Édifié sur une ancienne arène circulaire elle-même insérée dans un bastion pentagonal de Vauban datant du XVIIᵉ siècle, ce bâtiment rond se présente sous la forme d'un anneau de 75 mètres de diamètre. Les architectes expliquent que bien que le travail sur ce site ait été difficile, ils pensent avoir réussi à montrer la présence de l'architecture originelle, et ce même si leur construction est entièrement neuve. C'est en particulier le cas de l'espace central dont la fonction a été comme renversée puisqu'il s'agissait d'amener le public dans cet espace jadis affecté aux taureaux. Le vide est entouré d'anneaux de polyester qui donnent l'impression que les limites de l'espace se dissolvent dans la lumière. La construction est en béton, acier et profilés de fibre de verre et de polycarbonate pour les anneaux extérieurs, en tubes de Plexiglas blanc de 12 cm de diamètre pour le cylindre principal et en panneaux de polycarbonate pour les murs et le plafond de l'auditorium principal. Pour les architectes « ce tour de magie », l'indétermination apparente de cet énorme vide, n'a été possible que grâce à l'implantation en sous-sol d'une bonne partie des équipements du programme. L'intérieur est traité de façon similaire à l'aide de matériaux translucides et d'un oculus central qui éclaire le centre du bâtiment. Plus ils travaillaient sur la légèreté et la transparence de centre de conférences plus les architectes avaient l'impression de prendre en charge et de perpétuer l'histoire de ce site si particulier.

The encircling wall of polyester rings visible above gives an inscrutable lightness to the architecture, in a sense creating a false façade.

Die oben zu sehende Umfassungswand aus Polyesterringen, die in gewissem Sinn wie eine Scheinfassade wirkt, verschafft der Architektur eine feinsinnige Leichtigkeit.

Le mur de clôture en anneaux de polyester, visible ci-dessus, confère une légèreté impalpable à l'architecture en dressant presque une fausse façade.

The elegance of the design is highlighted in these images showing an entrance canopy (above) and a large pivoting door (below). The overall site view below shows the center as a kind of enigmatic object in the midst of a relatively unattractive urban environment.

Die Eleganz dieses Entwurfs kommt auf den Bildern des Eingangsvordachs (oben) und der großformatigen Drehtür (unten) gut zur Geltung. Auf der Gesamtansicht des Geländes wirkt das Zentrum wie ein rätselhaftes Objekt inmitten eines eher öden urbanen Umfelds.

L'élégance du projet est mise en valeur dans ces images qui montrent l'auvent de l'entrée (ci-dessus) et une grande porte pivotante (ci-dessous). La vue d'ensemble fait du centre une sorte d'objet énigmatique au milieu d'un environnement urbain peu séduisant.

As appears to be frequently the case in contemporary Spanish architecture, Selgas Cano here contrasts the external lightness of the building with a floating, but almost menacing volume of concrete within the structure.

Wie so häufig in der aktuellen Architektur Spaniens kontrastiert Selgas Cano hier die äußere Leichtigkeit des Gebäudes mit einer schwebenden, fast bedrohlichen Betonmasse im Inneren des Gebäudes.

Comme souvent en architecture contemporaine espagnole, Selgas Cano joue du contraste entre la légèreté apparente du bâtiment et le poids du volume suspendu presque menaçant du fait du béton qu'il contient.

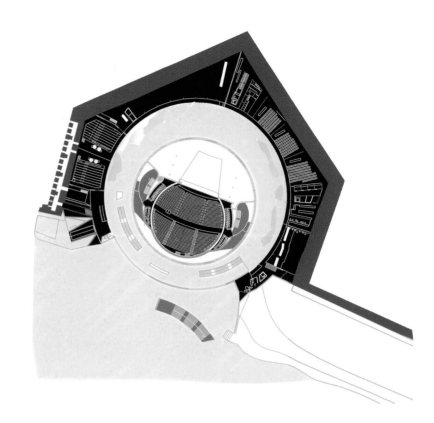

PHOTO CREDITS IMPRINT

CREDITS PHOTOS / PLANS / DRAWINGS / CAD DOCUMENTS

18–23 top, 24–25 © Roland Halbe/artur / 23 bottom © Ábalos & Herreros / 26–31 top and bottom, 32 top, 33–36 top and bottom, 37 top, 38 bottom, 39–41 top right and bottom © Roland Halbe/artur / 31 middle, 32 bottom, 36 middle, 37 bottom, 38 top, 41 top left © Eduardo Arroyo/NO.MAD Arquitectos, S. L. / 42–46 bottom, 47 top–50 bottom, 51 top, 52 top, 53 © Alan Karchmer / 46 top, 47 bottom, 50 top, 51 bottom, 52 bottom, 56 bottom, 57 top © Santiago Calatrava / 55, 56 top, 57 bottom–59 © Nick Guttridge/VIEW/artur / 60–64 top left and bottom, 65–68 top, 69 © Fernando Alda / 64 top right, 68 bottom © Estudio Alberto Campo Baeza / 70–75 © S. Cirugeda / 76–80 top, 81 bottom, 82–86 top, 87 bottom–89 © Roland Halbe/artur / 80 bottom, 81 top, 86 bottom, 87 top, 89 bottom right © Anton Garcia-Abril & Ensamble Studio / 90–97 top © Roland Halbe/artur / 97 bottom © Rafael de La-Hoz Arquitectos / 98–102 bottom, 103 top © Duccio Malagamba / 102 top, 103 bottom © Josep Llinàs / 104, 108–109 top © Roland Halbe/artur / 107, 110 top–114 bottom, 115 © César San Millan / 109 bottom, 110 bottom, 114 top © Francisco Mangado / 116–121 bottom, 123 © Roland Halbe/artur / 122 top and bottom Luis Asin © Mansilla + Tuñón Arquitectos / 121 top, 122 middle © Mansilla + Tuñón Arquitectos / 124–129 top, 130–134 top left and bottom, 135 top © Roland Halbe/artur / 129 bottom, 134 top right, 135 bottom © Fernando Menis/AMP Arquitectos / 136–141 top, 142–143 bottom © Roland Halbe/artur / 141 bottom, 143 top © Miralles Tagliabue EMBT / 144 top, 147–148 top, 149 bottom left © Roland Halbe/artur / 144 bottom, 148 bottom, 149 bottom right © Duccio Malagamba / 149 top © Rafael Moneo / 150–154 bottom, 155 top–158 top, 159 © Roland Halbe/artur / 154 top, 155 bottom, 158 bottom © Nieto Sobejano Arquitectos S. L. / 160–165, 166 top left and bottom, 167 top © Roland Halbe/artur / 164 top, 166 top right, 167 bottom © Paredes Pedrosa Arquitectos / 168–173 top and bottom, 174 top, 175 top, 177–178 top, 179 top and bottom, 180 top left and bottom, 181 top–183 © Hisao Suzuki / 173 middle, 174 bottom, 175 bottom, 178 bottom, 179 middle, 180 top right, 181 bottom © RCR Aranda Pigem Vilalta Arquitectes / 184–190 bottom, 191 © Roland Halbe/artur / 190 top © José Selgas y Lucia Cano Arquitectos

To stay informed about upcoming TASCHEN titles, please request our magazine at www.taschen.com/magazine or write to TASCHEN, Hohenzollernring 53, D-50672 Cologne, Germany, contact@taschen.com, Fax: +49-221-254919. We will be happy to send you a free copy of our magazine which is filled with information about all of our books.

© VG Bild-Kunst, Bonn 2007,
for the works of Eduardo Arroyo and Santiago Calatrava

© 2007 TASCHEN GmbH
Hohenzollernring 53, D-50672 Köln
www.taschen.com

PROJECT MANAGEMENT: Florian Kobler, Cologne
COLLABORATION: Mischa Gayring, Cologne
PRODUCTION: Thomas Grell, Cologne
DESIGN: Sense/Net, Andy Disl and Birgit Reber, Cologne
GERMAN TRANSLATION: Christiane Court, Frankfurt/M
FRENCH TRANSLATION: Jacques Bosser, Paris

Printed in Italy
ISBN 978-3-8228-5261-3